T0150050

I expected a book about Mark Anthony's life as a funeral director but "Living and Dying" is so much more. This is a book about life! By sharing stories from his personal journey, Mark shows us how he overcame adversity and found peace by learning to live through his heart instead of trying to think his way through life. Mark's sincere desire to help make the world a better place is evident throughout this book.

—*John Callaghan*
Chief Business Strategist, FuneralSuccess.com
Founder, The Center for Business Transformation

It is the rare funeral director who understands how to serve grieving families with genuine empathy and lives an open-hearted, on-purpose life, personally and professionally. Such a funeral director makes a transformative difference in the lives of thousands. Such a funeral director as Mark Anthony. His words of wisdom in this insightful book will help thereaders befriend loss, grief, and death so that they might truly live their precious days here on earth.

—*Dr. Alan D. Wolfelt*
Author, Educator, Grief Counselor
Director, Center for Loss and Life Transition

Encourager, Courageous, Bold, Compassionate, Interesting. These are words that come to mind as I reflect on my experience with Mark Anthony's latest work...and it is an experience as much as it is enlightenment.

Each of us, as children, have hopes and dreams. Men aspire to be heroes and admired, Women (I think) aspire to be loved and beautiful. As adults, life is often something less than we had hoped. Thoreaux once said: "Most men lead lives of quiet desperation." But, for Mark Anthony, accepting such a statement would be giving up.

In a remarkably courageous and bold style he leads us on his own life journey as a funeral director, but more important… a man. It takes courage as a man to be as open and vulnerable as Mr. Anthony is. But, in so doing, he gives the reader permission to be open and vulnerable. And it is in that open and vulnerable place that we are able to find purpose, our meaning and ourselves.

Thank you, Mark, for leading the way.

—*Alan Creedy*
Author of "The Creedy Commentary"
http://funeralhomeconsulting.org/

Early in my graduate training, a wise professor told our group of students, "Principles are borne best on the wings of a story." Living and Dying: Finding Love & Hope in the Journey of Loss", my colleague and friend, Mark Anthony, follows the seasoned professor's advice. With warmth, compassion, candor, and humor, Mark weaves together a tapestry that considers death, consolation, family struggles, abandonment, joy, pure love, and a host of other human experiences. Though this little volume is filled with spiritual musings, his storytelling never resorts to a "preachy" tone. Instead, he gently leads readers through a careful consideration of what it means to make deep, loving connections—with our families, our friends, our colleagues, and our world. In a day when there is so much incivility in public speech, his words are a breath of fresh air, as calming as a warm summer breeze.

—*Dr. William G. Hoy, FT*
Clinical Professor of Medical Humanities
Baylor University

Mark Anthony has written a book that is so unique, you will never read another like it. He's a funeral director. But it's not a book about "My life within the funeral profession," or "Behind the scenes in the funeral business," or even his musings on how he copes with his profession. The title says it well. It's about living and dying.

Mark is not a man who has numbed himself against the emotions of his work. He knows to approach it with care, but he hasn't reduced it to just the mechanical workings. Instead, in some miraculous way, he seems to have experienced every day's work as a new immersion.

This is a clear and direct exposition of what he's come to believe about life during this exceptional, eyes-wide-open stream of experience in dealing with death. The intensity of it has drawn him in to the roots and branches of our families, our strengths and weaknesses, our days of clarity, our nights of blindness. He has found interest and learning in unexpected places, and brings them to our attention. And he shows us important differences in the way we live and die. He states his conclusions, too.

Very directly. You won't agree with all of his beliefs, but he rarely advocates, he just states. And he does it in a way that forces you to consider what he says. To properly set this in motion, you'll hear the story of his past. You will know him well as someone similar to yourself. This will immediately create in you the impact of walking into a life that might frighten many of us. And here you will get the perspective of an individual—most importantly, an inspired one.

I'm happy that I didn't miss this book. My reaction upon finishing it was that I'm so glad I read it at this point in my life. And you'll be grateful for the effect of it at any point in yours. You should get to reading it now.

—*Bob Cannan*
CEO, Eagle Productivity Solutions
http://eagleproductivity.com

Mark has opened up to show his true heart. Everyone will be able to move one step closer to healing when they read this thoughtful life story. This book guides the reader through an impossible time with a story, gesture or touch of the hand.

—*Mark Cuddy*
Director of Membership Development
Selected Independent Funeral Home

Being on one side of grief and looking in on another was beautiful! Thank you!

—*Judy Leman*

It has been said that smart people give lessons while wise people tell stories. Mark Anthony creates multiple paths of conversation from the center of his own experience with loss and grief. This book is a wheel, asking the reader to turn the mind and spirit as the wheel turns toward topics related to life, loss, spirit, mind, belief, faith, connection, reflection, celebration, healing. In a sense, Anthony has assembled an articulate mandala, a microcosm of the universe, an image of the cosmos, an affirmation of life growing, by measures, through struggle, impediments, and grief. This book is a meeting place of science and theology, traditional culture and recent innovations, religious rituals and emotional need. But it is, first and foremost, a personal testimony offered in compelling story. It is Mark Anthony's story, and his ruminations about life, loss, rituals surrounding death, and the emotional connections that build and support human community. In Romans 14:19, the Apostle Paul offers this: "Let us then pursue what makes for peace and for mutual upbuilding. "Living and Dying: Finding Love & Hope in the Journey of Loss" is an extension of this same invitation. Readers from all walks of life will be enriched, and communities will be strengthened, and healing of the bereaved will take place because Mark Anthony has chosen to tell his story.

—*The Rev'd Dr. W. Kenneth Williams*
Retired Pastor, First Baptist Church, Rochester, NY
Chaplain Emeritus
Brighton Fire Department, Rochester, NY

Having served in pastoral work for over three decades, I've experienced the various encounters. I've cherished the smiles. Rejoicing with those who are celebrating life's seasons of birth, marriage, dedication, baptism, relational restoration, home safely from war, and good news from the doctor. The meals, the laughter, the music, the applause, the peace. Sadness, though, has visited often. Not all news from the doctor is good. Not all soldiers return home. Not all gatherings are flavored with joy. Disappointments, disabilities, debt, and death: the list is large of moments when we weep together.

So what should we do? Refuse to talk about those times? I say, address those movements. Learn from them. Find healthy methods of living through and experiencing hope during life's storms.

Here is a guide to help us do that when living with grief. The author, Mark Anthony, directs us toward preparing for death—not in theory or theology, but in practical steps of gaining a healthy view of death and completing assignments during the process. Preparing funerals, discussing preferences, and seeing death through a better view are included in Mark's honest, creative work. Do not miss this chance to prepare now for the death of someone you love. And do not miss obtaining the knowledge of a much better life we can all live in the present.

—*Chris Maxwell*
Director of Spiritual Life
Author, Epilepsy Advocate
www.chrismaxwell.mes

LIVING & DYING

LIVING&
DYING

NDING LOVE & HOPE IN
HE JOURNEY OF LOSS

MARK K. ANTHONY

PUBLISHING & MARKETING

Oviedo, Florida

Living & Dying: Finding Love & Hope in the Journey of
Loss

Published by
HigherLife Publishing & Marketing Inc.
PO Box 623307
Oviedo, FL 32762
www.ahigherlife.com

Hardback ISBN: 978-0-9978018-1-1
ebook ISBN: 978-0-9978018-2-8

Cover design: David Whitlock

First Edition
17 18 19 20 21 22 — 9 8 7 6 5 4 3 2 1
Printed in the United States of America

Dedication

I would like to dedicate this book to the many families I have had the privilege to serve in the funeral profession. Their hard work as they journeyed through their grief has been an inspiration to me. Without the passion for life and the challenges of our life together, none of this would be possible.

Table of Contents

Acknowledgements

I would like to express my heartfelt thanks to my wife and children for their continued passion and energy they emit every day in the care and support of the families we serve.

Introduction

U p until now this has only been a thought—the thought to write a book. I believe that, for me, writing helps connect the intuitive mind and cognitive mind, and creates a clearer path toward understanding. Writing enhances the ability to teach or reproduce the needed idea and to bring forth its truth, or to manifest a perceived reality.

As it is for many of us, I didn't realize how much I have to offer. When you're living your everyday life, your everyday thoughts and ideas seem pretty ordinary—or even petty. How could my thoughts or ideas have any impact on the world and those around me? When I informed some good friends that "I" was writing a book, I received a few surprising reactions. The first was, "Are you an English major?" This was an easy question to answer. With today's technology, editing, formatting, and even self-publishing, producing a book is relatively easy.

The second reaction I received, more importantly, was; "What would you have to say that would be of interest to others?" That thought hit me like a ton of bricks; I felt that my answer to this had to be much more significant. Most of us believe that we do don't have much to offer our world which is a fundamental problem in our personal growth. The question challenged my mind most of that night as I tossed and turned. I realized that I was not entirely sure if I really did have something to offer.

The next morning, I awoke with the answer. I am so grateful today for being asked this tough question because it helped me realize just how important it is for me to write this book.

Struggle:

> *"Struggle is the food from which change is made, and the best time to make the most of a struggle is when it's right in front of your face. Now, I know that might sound a bit simplistic. But, too often we're led to believe that struggling is a bad thing, or that we struggle because we're doing something*

wrong. I disagree. I look at struggle as an opportunity to grow. True struggle happens when you can sense what is not working for you and you're willing to take the appropriate action to correct the situation. Those who accomplish change are willing to engage the struggle."

—Danny Dreyer[1]

I believe it is our calling and responsibility to take on these challenges and manage them to whatever degree we are capable.

I like Danny Dreyer's comment, "I look at struggle as an opportunity to grow. True struggle happens when you can sense what is not working for you and you're willing to take the appropriate action to correct the situation. Those who accomplish change are willing to engage the struggle."

I have had the opportunity to be challenged by many obstacles, difficulties, and struggles in my life and career. It is the way I have dealt with these

---

1 https://www.goodreads.com/author/quotes/222634.Danny_Dreyer

struggles that is the underlying purpose of this book. I use the word opportunity because I can see now how these struggles have been the catalyst for my journey and my growth. I can see now that these shared struggles and thoughts can also be a catalyst for others' growth as well.

My knowledge, my truths, and the very nature and meaning of life revolve around a world very few wish to examine, the death of a loved one. While I get asked the question frequently "How can one do the work you do?" the answer is always the same.

First, in order to do this work you need to care about people. Isn't that a great thing to have to focus on every day?

Second, I recognize it's a privilege and honor to be invited into a family's private lives when they are their most vulnerable.

And last, one cannot exist and work in this environment without a strong spiritual foundation on which to stand. Organized religion and my church experience, although valuable, could not offer me the personal experience that my everyday professional life has provided, an experience for which I am very grateful.

I have spent most of my time examining and questioning everything. Perhaps this is a result of my broken family or my perfectionist, controlling nature, or more accurately, my strong desire to be the best I can be. I hope to take you through the process of thought and heartfelt feelings, through my stories and reflections on many issues and topics. They come from all aspects of my experience over the past forty plus years (of my sixty years) in or around the funeral profession. Some of these thoughts and stories will challenge you in many ways, while others may seem insignificant. You will all recognize them because I believe we all touch upon similar issues in many ways, at varying levels and degrees in our life. It is because of my sincere love for this life and the opportunities that life brings that I share my thoughts, my heart and my love for you, the reader.

While we may not be able to change the reaction of others in our world, we are able to change our own reaction to it. It is my hope, that through knowledge, experience and trust we can build a bridge together. By knowing that we are not alone, that we are all connected and "in it" together, we all can contribute to the outcome. If we only see hatred, trials, and tribulations, we will live in a world of despair and suffering. If we see opportunity, love, and hope, we will live in a world of joy and gratitude.

This is why I needed to write this book: To establish a connection of hope, love and a passion for caring and healing in our world. I will keep you in my thoughts and prayers. Please do the same for me.

Chapter One

Hope

*"You didn't come into this world. You
came out of it, like a wave from the
ocean. You are not a stranger here."*
—*Alan Watts*

As I reflect on my life's journey I can see
how my intuitive nature has been a loving,
caring and supportive companion along
its path. I have experienced it through my imagination, creativity, love of life, and spiritual reflection.
As Alan Watts says "you are not a stranger here," I
believe him.

I have always loved the imaginative, intuitive
mind. When revealed, it brings such connection
and clarity for me. This connection has further led

me to an awareness of something both profound and tangible. I refer to this awareness as the source. Whether you prefer to identify "source" as God, the Tao, Buddha, the Divine, Consciousness, or by any other name is completely your choice. This connection can and will open up the world and universe in its entirety to us as we connect individually and as a whole. It can be said that all beings or experiences are connected this way. If we were to simplify our lives, strip away our thoughts, judgments and fears for just a moment we would realize how easy it is to make this connection. If we were to accept this process of surrendering and trusting, we would learn and experience that all we need to do or know will be revealed to us.

These words remind me of the story of the man who falls from a cliff only to grab a limb thereby saving him from a painful demise. After many repeated calls for help and as the limb begins to unearth itself, a voice finally responds to his plea for help. The voice identifies itself as the Lord and replies that all the man needs to do is trust in him, surrender and let go. After a long pause you hear the man's response, "Is there anyone else up there?"

Imagine the freedom that would result in not having the binds or constraints of the outer mind and being able to just trust, surrender and connect with our source? For many years I have known about this connection and its feeling, but have been fooled into believing that my mental powers were more suited to the physical world. With my mental powers I could control, manipulate, and overcome many obstacles in this world. It took many years of intense effort to produce the results wanted. And yet, truly, were the results worth the costs and were they what I really wanted?

There have been many good things that have happened to me and our business. Many good things as a result of hard work, dedication and a passion for caring—not control or manipulation. This is why I wish to make this effort of writing and sharing the thoughts that have accompanied me on my journey, I believe that the insights that I have gained on this journey can be experienced by anyone who is willing to connect to the source.

What is truly remarkable to me is how we either

feel or do not feel connection. We can feel connected through family, friends, work, social, and cultural experiences. We are designed to feel connected emotionally, spiritually, mentally and physically. Our shared connection can feel intensely good, yet there are days when we feel completely alone. How can that be? What is it that disconnects us? Where does the connection go? Is it a physical disconnect? Are we hurting so badly that the energy needed to connect is hidden and blocked? Is it an emotional disconnection? Is it so bad sometimes that our anger, or fear, blocks our ability to communicate our thoughts? Or is it a spiritual disconnect, where we feel completely separate in our growth and our faith? Do we often feel lost and utterly disappointed with God for not helping us find our way and/or answering our prayers? I believe it's all of the above, and I have experienced it all just as you have.

There are many great books and speakers talking about a new age, a new phase in our world. The main theme of these books revolves around the concept of returning to our source or connecting with our source. What I'm most happy about these days is that the more people I listen to, the more I am hearing the same thing. This is a time filled with struggle, fear, and trepidation. Yet it is exciting to see these things as they are slowly being eroded by love. The world is emerging to a new place as if a cloud has been removed from our heavens, as if something is uncovering new truths about the universe, as if there is a new and strengthened connection. It is undeniably a very powerful and transforming time—albeit extreme at times.

With all types of connection there is an internal experience or reaction that either feels foreign and odd, or good and right. While I believe we all have a common spiritual connection and a lot of what I write about reflects that idea, there are many other ways in which we connect. In fact, the mere experience of reading these words connects us in a world of thought, and that experience, that thought will undoubtedly create an energy that is felt as emotion. I know that for some, the words on these pages will produce an emotional response. I know that for some, the words on these pages will cause disagreement and reaction. I know that for some, the words on these pages will move them to a new place of understanding. I know that the mere fact that we react to being connected in any way is the purpose of our lives.

The goal of this book is not only to introduce my ideas, but to also have the reader participate by releasing their emotional energy into the world, bringing hope, love and compassion to a world that desperately needs it. It can only be hoped that this effort in some way will enhance my experience and the experience of all who cross my path.

It is with great humility that I continue to move forward on this path toward connection. Life is a journey that is unique to each of us and I am grateful for all that has happened to bring me here.

My tears are tears of joy, for they come from a place of connection, the love and the beauty of what we experience together.

Chapter Two

Joy

"Your deepest roots are in nature. No matter who you are, where you live, or what kind of life you lead, you remain irrevocably linked with the rest of creation."
—Charles Cook

Over the years, the funeral profession has brought me to places I never imagined I would be. I am routinely asked to enter into situations where the family unit is under great stress, at a time when the pain and strain on the family is at an extreme. I am asked to help people travel down a road that even I have not yet traveled. Day after day, there are new situations, new personalities, new pains, struggles and new stories. I've been directed to answer the big questions about life and death. At times, I have struggled with how to bring these ideas into my everyday life for those that I serve. It's been like a master class in life, but after over thirty-five years I realize that it has taken its toll. My body is sacrifically scarred from the emotional and physical trauma of people's lives. Yet at this point in my life, I somehow feel a strength and resolve, a new resurgence of energy and renewal. Although my body can't take the pace as it once did, it has found a new rhythm and a new song to sing—and it is good. It is about passion, direction, movement, and love of our connection. In this new place there have been many new lessons, new awakenings and sense of peace. The old adage, "energy follows thought," rings very true for me. Whatever I put my attention on is brought forth, whether it is lack or abundance, pain or joy.

> *My body is sacrifically scarred from the emotional and physical trauma of people's lives. Yet at this point in my life, I somehow feel a strength and resolve, a new resurgence of energy and renewal.*

Joy

I had the experience of living in joy for two weeks around the time of my sixtieth birthday. I like to tell the story of a dream I had at that time, which is where the experience began. In the dream, I was having breakfast with my two-year-old grandson at my favorite diner. He looked to me when he saw a bird fly by and asked me, "Ba Ba," (he calls me Ba Ba,) and he really couldn't talk in real life, "how come birds can fly?" My response was, "Because it's their nature." After a reflective pause in the conversation, I then asked my grandson, "What is our nature?" His immediate response was, "Our nature's to love, Ba Ba" and then went casually back to eating his breakfast. As I let that moment of childhood innocence and powerful truth flow over and through me, an overwhelming feeling of love and joy filled my being. I could only think of one thing so I asked him, "How come so many of us don't follow our nature?" He said, "It's because we can think. Animals can't think and when you can think, you can forget."

The dream brought me to tears for weeks after as I truly saw only love everywhere and for everyone I came into contact with. Whether it was the checkout girl at the register, the gas attendant, my family, or friends, I could only feel joy and love for everyone, I was love in its fullest. It was during that time when I realized that we all have the choice to shape our experience into what it is that we want, and only we can make that happen for ourselves.

Weeks later I returned to the other world, the back and forth world of love and fear. Often when I felt removed from love, I would notice a sense of being lost which made me angry, unloving and in some way less than I wanted to be and feel. It was in this struggle with loss that I became aware of my own loss of connection.

When I felt lost I would spend time in my head trying to figure it all out. Why was it happening? What was wrong with me? Why, why, why? It was this back and forth activity 'life' that brought me to this place today.

What I learned and continue to learn is all of our struggles are merely opportunities for re-direction, re-orienting us to find our path. They are really a blessing, a gift. I soon realized that when I felt lost, it was only because I had lost my way—taken a detour off the main highway. Because it was such a frequent event in my life, I just didn't really notice it.

The experience of those two weeks of pure love and joy brought me to a place where I now recognize more frequently that feeling of disconnection—and I don't like it. If we can find a way to re-orient our attention with our source, getting back to that main highway, when we feel these things, we can find our way back. We can return to the place that connects us with all things in our universe, a perpetual energy zone where all things are possible. Maybe all we need is a good map!

Chapter Three

Thoughts

"Look! Look! Look deep into nature and
you will understand everything."
—Albert Einstein

The connection exists, whether we are tuned in to it or not, between each and everything that has or ever will exist. Our willingness to feel connected is all that is required.

The connection I feel with my son, Michael, is one example that comes to mind as to how powerful our connection is. Michael lives in Montana and as a smoke jumper, he is part of an elite group of highly trained professionals that jump from airplanes into remote areas of our country to extinguish wild fires. As a mom and a dad we had many opportunities to think of him as we imagined all sorts of dangerous and exciting adventures. Not all wonderful thoughts as friends would call us after hearing of the devastating news of an entire fire crew dying as they fought wildfires out west.

As I sit here right now in the safety and warmth of my home in upstate New York, I can connect my mind and heart with his whole being, simply by bringing the complete idea of him into my thoughts and consciousness. Simply by closing my eyes and letting all other thoughts and distractions go, I can connect with the idea that represents Michael in my mind. Inside my mind, this idea of Michael really "is" Michael. I can see him and sense his presence in my imagination. It is my idea of him that makes him real, not his physical presence. And I can do that whether he is physically here or not, and whenever I want. In that place, we are totally connected in my mind and heart just as though—he is sitting right here with me now. The connection may not be able to put us together physically, but we are never separated, the connection exists.

If you were to put this book down right now and

think of someone you care deeply for, they too can come fully into your awareness.

Close your eyes.

Take a moment to visualize that person. Feel and sense their presence.

Although they may be a great distance from you, you have the ability to connect with them.

We all see and experience this connection as it appears through our memories that are connected to things and places. I, for one, cannot walk past a Cinnabon food station at the airport without bringing back to mind my grandmother. The images of these wonderful brown sugar coated cinnamon rolls and their smell remind me how much I loved both Nana and her cinnamon rolls. Likewise, your memories of certain songs and favorite places can transport you to a very specific place and time. Pictures, sounds, and smells all have the ability to return us to a place in our memory that connects us with a certain time, person, or place. My own memories of the six months I spent visiting my dad in a rehab center after a life changing accident come flooding back to me as soon as I smell and experience any hospital lobby.

In the event of loss, family members that live past their partner's lifespan feel this connection regularly. Imagine the typical morning you now spend with your partner. You wake up in the morning, make the coffee, get the paper and sit down in front of the daily news show. For forty, fifty, or maybe even sixty years this is been the routine many of us share with our spouse. But imagine that today they are not there with you. While they may not be there physically, in our hearts and minds they are there. That is our connection—it's been our pattern, our reality. Spouses often say that they may even pour a second cup of coffee, only to remember there is no one there to drink it. They find themselves driving to the hospital where they have been visiting for many weeks, only to remember they don't need to go there anymore. The routines that have been ingrained in our minds take weeks, months, or even years in some cases to re-orient. If we take a look at our mind and consider how it works, we realize that all of our thoughts are based on memories and experiences. We rely on the constant access our minds have to our memory banks of information that guide us through the day. We do this without any conscious knowledge of it. Our bodies are conditioned to run on automatic pilot and maneuver through the obstacle course of life.

Ladies and gentlemen, boys and girls!!! We are not going CRAZY! We are doing exactly what we are programmed to do. I cannot say that loud enough. We are not going crazy. We do not need drugs; we do not need to fear. All we really need to do is to be kind to ourselves, take our time, and learn to appreciate and understand our connection. Connect to our memories, tell the story, remember, laugh and cry, and whatever it is that you are moved to do. There is no right or wrong here, there is only right, for you.

I am sure this theme will be repeated over and over again and if not, shame on me.

Chapter Four

Responsibility

"Man is not himself only...He is all that he sees; all that flows to him from a thousand sources...He is the land, the lift of its mountain lines, the reach of its valleys."
—Mary Austin

In my early years, the programming I received was deeply affected by a trauma in my parents' life.

My dad married the love of his life in his early twenties. I was a product of this union, and have little memory or evidence of what happened but I know it wasn't good. In fact, I have never seen any pictures of my mom and dad together and no pictures of me with them. In fact, the only memory I have of her is in her apartment when I was about four or five years old. I can remember listening to the classical musical recording of "Peter and the Wolf," and I recall the aroma and scent of her perfume. As the story goes,

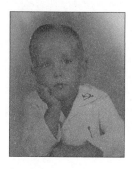 my mother wanted my dad to leave his family's controlling ways and leave town to start their own life. Family bonds can be both a curse and a blessing. In this case it destroyed their relationship, eventually leading to legal action over my custody. Although not customary in the 1950s, my father gained custody of me. I believe this may have been due to some character assassination of my mother and her family that caused her to leave town and, more importantly me, to start her life over. As I'm sure you can imagine it was not a good time in our family and many of us were permanently scarred by this event (more to follow).

Although my early memories are few, the images I hold of my mom are still, to this day, very poignant and intense. I actually have come to learn of the

strong bond between a mother and child, and I know that it is a connection that always exists no matter what the circumstances. As for my relationship with my dad, it was a connection that I'm sure hurt him deeply every time he looked at me, not something he could forget or 'get over.' I remained a physical reminder of the connection he felt with my mother.

At three years old I was placed in my grandmother's care and she raised me until my dad remarried when I was six years old. I can remember many good times living with my grandmother. She loved me and helped me feel safe. I remember a specific exercise I performed every night as I was put to sleep. I would take my pillow and blanket and lay at the base of the bedroom door so I could hear the voices in the house. It did not make it easy to enter the room but I wasn't stupid. I was not going to be left again.

My new mom was a schoolteacher and had a decent handle on dealing with kids, but never really allowed a connection with me. I believe it was my father that kept her removed from me for some selfish reason—like I was off limits. My new mom couldn't get close and show her love for me, and my dad couldn't say or confront it. I was on my own again. She and my dad had two boys and life was relatively good for all of us.

My dad was an amazing guy in many ways, and we had a good life as kids. My childhood memories include camping, summering at the lake, and playing in the neighborhood. My connection with my family was always strained by the memory of where I came from and the pain associated with it, but it was okay. I believe that somewhere around the age of five or six I found my direction in life. I took on the job of spiritual leader, or keeper, of my dad and the family as a whole. It felt like I was being offered the key to the kingdom. I felt true happiness, joy, and love. I can actually recall the peace and the feeling of connection I had at the age of five that has not changed over the years, but it has been clouded at times. In fact, if you look at a picture of me at five, you can physically see it.

A good exercise for all of us is to find a picture of us at the age of around five. Most likely you, too, will see yourself as you truly are, free of responsibility, fear, and judgment. We were all born into this.

Wilma Rudolph (the Olympic athlete) is quoted as saying "Never underestimate the power of dreams and the influence of the human spirit. We are all the same in this notion: The potential for greatness lives within each of us."

I had experienced this notion, but what eventually changed is what I did with it. I did the same thing that most of us do with it—we take it and make it our responsibility. We take it and try to manage it, control it, categorize and manipulate it. We take it and literally destroy its beauty, peace and joy. We make it our personal responsibility.

Chapter Five

Control

*"Away from the tumult of motor and
mill I want to be carefree;
I want to be still!
I'm weary of doing things; weary of Words I
want to be one with the blossoms and birds."*
—Edgar A. Guest

My dad had a life changing accident at fifty-two years old leaving him in a wheelchair paralyzed from his mid chest down. He was at our cottage where there was a tree limb blocking the view to the north. As he sawed away at the mighty oak tree limb, he passed out and dropped forty feet down the bank to the lakeshore. His wife, mother, and sister were all sitting on the screened in porch as he vaulted the bank. For what seemed like an eternity, he lay unconscious on the bank until he stopped breathing. It was literally seconds later that the volunteer fire department and

medics arrived on the scene. He was brought back to life and then transferred to the local hospital to be stabilized. I met him in the city that night at the university medical center to experience the drama and meet with the

spinal cord trauma team. To say that hospitals can be a scary place is an understatement. I experienced the full spectrum of life altering decisions and conversations during those hours immediately following the accident. It was only after the third day that the hospital's neurosurgeon informed my dad that he would never walk again.

As the oldest son and the one who had made it my responsibility to care for my father years ago, even I was challenged. Overnight, I became a major player in my family's funeral business as well as the guardian of their finances and well-being. The major obstacles increased tenfold. Handicapped accessibility became a necessity at home and work. Mobility, credibility, sensibility, even the most basic hygiene and daily activities required reorienting. For a time, it was basically hell on earth. My connection was being challenged on all levels. For some with loss from a disability there seems a need to take out their frustrations on someone. I was the dutiful son and it was I that took the brunt of my father's frustrations. I was the one who was called at two in the morning to help him back into bed or his wheelchair. I was the one that was there every day to assist and support him. I was the one who was there to take the full brunt of his anger, pain, and the fear he felt as a result of his loss, GRIEF!!

This brings me to my point. My relationship with my dad through those years had become so damaging and so difficult to manage on top of all the other control needs that I couldn't, or more truthfully, I didn't want to do it anymore. What I was beginning to learn was that having control is a decision produced by the mind and it was my choice as to what to do about it. The mind is designed for control and it is very good at it, but at the point at which it's allowed to overrule the heart is where the needed connection breaks down. We all have our breaking points in relationships where the burden of responsibility weighs heavy and we decide to change it.

I chose to become my dad's advisor, offering my thoughts on how he should fix himself in his new journey as a paraplegic. Through my decision to be responsible for his fixing, I, in essence, became his parent in the family model. I suggested that he learn to read. I suggested that he develop new interests in computers, hobbies etc. Our roles reversed, and I essentially stopped being the loving son and became a demanding parent. Frustrations grew and eventually our relationship became one of painful avoidance. I finally made a conscious decision to end the relationship I had created with my father. It took me many years but on the day of his death thirteen years later, I was 95% complete with finalizing our relationship. I completed the remaining 5% required to end the relationship during the twenty minutes the EMT's spent working to revive my dad in the living room of his house.

What I did for those twenty minutes was to grieve at a level I had not experienced before. I merely sat there and cried harder and deeper than I knew was possible. I was saying goodbye to a painful, distrustful and hurtful relationship. It was the most cleansing cry I had ever experienced. In twenty minutes alone in the room, I spoke to my dad and I told him everything I wanted to say. I told him how I loved him, how sad I was for the hurt and the suffering he had experienced in his life and how much I wished it could have been different. I told him how I hoped that he could find peace in his journey.

I'll share a story later about the power of being exhausted, but the twenty-minute cry was one of the most exhausting twenty minutes I've ever had and probably one of the most satisfying. I walked out of his house and followed the ambulance to the hospital where he was pronounced dead. We had both reached an emotional place of relief—or perhaps a better word is release—that day. My dad, who had faced struggles and challenges in his life, was free from all of them.

I was too.

It was liberating. In that moment it felt as if God had dropped in and said, "George, I'm going to take you out of the game. You have worked hard but it is time to take the bench. I'm going to give you a rest." "Mark, you get a vacation. Go try and figure out how you could have done better. Get back to work on who I designed you to be not what you think others want you to be or who you think you should be. Do the work and get back to me."

> *My connection was back. My heart and head were balanced. There was no fight to be had. All was well.*

My connection was back. My heart and head were balanced. There was no fight to be had. All was well.

The next few days and the years following that day have been focused not only on the blessing he was in my life, but also on my life's journey that was laid out before me. I became one with the blossoms and birds

Chapter Six

Freedom

"Nature is man's teacher.
She unfolds her treasure to his search,
Unseals his eye, illumes his mind,
and purifies his heart;
an influence breathes from all the sights and sounds
of her existence."
—*Alfred Billings Street*

S o let's talk about this connection, what is it and how do we know we're connected? For too many years I relied upon my mind to maneuver me through the day. I was on auto-pilot as discussed previously and I was exceptionally good at it. I was bright, interesting, engaging, challenging, and often simply amazing. My biggest dilemmas were obstacles thrown at me by the business, partners, employees, families I served in the funeral business, and my family, etc. I would revert to my mental abilities, the memories that had been programmed and saved to guide me through the minefield of life. Everywhere I went, there were bombs ready to go off and blow me off my path. I had already survived a lifetime of maneuvering life's landscape. I would tactically advance and retreat, advance and retreat, it was almost like a war to position myself on the RIGHT side.

A couple years after my dad's accident, my uncle (my dad's business partner) introduced the idea of his eldest son joining us in the business. I had experienced a baptism by fire after my dad's accident in that I had been the one called on to do his job, seeing families full time and running the funeral business. I was ready for the challenge but it was a struggle. I had a new wife and family of my own on the way, not to mention my dad's needs to contend with. Now, I was presented with the concept of another family member, my cousin, entering the business I had been a part of for seven years. I was concerned and felt the need to connect with what that would mean to me. The current buy and sell agreement at the time was that in the event of my dad's death, the stock would be purchased by my uncle. The business had become important to me and my dad's health was compromised by his paraplegia; I decided to begin the process of considering the purchase of my dad's stock in the business. I found an attorney and an accountant to represent me, and we went about the process of valuing the business.

We spent a good year discussing the potential sale, yet my dad was not in agreement to sell. My wife and I found ourselves with a decision to make. Should we weather the storm and hope that my dad wouldn't die? And that if he did, my uncle would do the right thing and that he would sell my dad's share of the business back to me? Or, should we take a stand and try to force the sale?

We decided to force the sale.

I went to my dad and told him if he didn't sell us his share, we were going to leave the business. To this day I don't believe we could have made that decision without having entered a place of connection.

We did it by researching, formulating a plan, and working together. We created a map, a plan, and a direction for our future. We didn't run away from it—we stood in the face of it and recognized it really didn't matter what happened and we would be OK with whatever happened. We knew that we would be fine because we were in it together. After I told my dad what I wanted and what I was prepared to do, he agreed. It was that easy.

In retrospect, I believe this action was reminiscent of what he had wanted to do as a young man when my mom pleaded with him to leave with her. Maybe he even respected me for forcing the issue. I'll never know; he never said.

Another story, illustrating the value of connection, is more recent. As my age advances it is time to begin the process of transferring ownership to the next generation at the funeral home. My business partner (my cousin) and I have been together since the early 1980s when we bought the business and we wanted to create a plan to transition ownership. We hired a consultant to assist in that process. It became clear very early on that my partner and I had issues in both personality and management styles. We had never shared a history of connection even after our childhood together. Because of our inability to deal with that, we instead shared a history of disagreement and dysfunction (one that our fathers had created before us). The consultant who worked with us over a year's time shared new ideas and offered suggestions to encourage mutual understanding and develop our relationship in a good and supportive way. During one of our meetings, she suggested to me that I needed to lead more with my heart and not my head.

You know when you have one of those moments in life where it all becomes clear? That was one of my big moments. I had always known about the connection between heart and head since I was a young boy, but now I was becoming an older man and it seemed to be the only thing that was important. I began practicing the art of leading with my heart. I would consider the person I was talking with to be the most important and interesting person in my life no matter where I was. I would consider that person to be the most interesting person in my life at that moment, and I would care. What I realized was that the head followed and was always present. Even though I might say the same things I would normally say, something was different. It felt different. People didn't react or fight back, they weren't afraid of me, and they would smile. They somehow felt and knew my heart was there.

This newfound communication was different and much more emotional. It was felt! It was not unlike the experience I'd had with joy around the time of my sixtieth birthday, and it was good.

Sometime during that discovery period, my partner and I were having our annual business meeting and we had one of our infamous yelling matches. Our advisors had seen this before and were great at getting us through our personal reactions. After that meeting, I was moved to do something different. I invited my partner to join me for lunch and a round of golf to further discuss any issues or concerns he felt we needed to attend to. I really wanted to care and listen because I wanted to lead with my heart. We had a great lunch that went on too long to play golf, and as I was driving out of the parking lot on my way home I had a revelation. This was the first time in over thirty years as partners that I'd had lunch with "my cousin," not my business partner. When I got home I found a picture with us and all our cousins on bicycles in the neighborhood.

This picture still hangs up in my home office. I can remember like yesterday all the years together as kids at the lake and the way his family had taken me in before my dad remarried. I remembered that we came from a place of connection, family first, and that whatever happened in business doesn't change that. There's no erasing family and the memories that are there. That's what leading with your heart does! It reconnects you with what is important; it opens the channel to caring, loving, and realizing what is "really" important. It is what is available to our world today. Author Alan Cohen is quoted as saying "We attain freedom as we let go of whatever does not reflect our magnificence. A bird cannot fly high or far with a stone tied to its back. But release the impediment, and we are free to soar to unprecedented heights."

Chapter Seven

Mission

"Never a day passes but that I do myself the honor to commune with some of nature's varied forms."
—*George Washington Carver*

Times are continually changing and I am spending some very focused and purposeful time establishing a new direction for our funeral business. It is obvious to me that we all need to focus on the connections in our relationships, with each other and ourselves. It is through this effort that we realize cooperation, and the opportunities for continued healing. It is also obvious to me that we must engage in experiencing the struggles and challenges in our life to maintain a healthy life.

Marcel Proust is quoted as saying, "We don't receive wisdom; we must discover it for ourselves after a journey that no one can take for us or spare us."

Our new vision/mission statement is CELEBRATE life, HONOR the journey, and HEAL the mind body and spirit. Everything we do has to resonate with any one or all of these concepts. Celebrate life means very clearly, LIFE in all of its conditions. Celebrate the experience, the love, the joy and peace, but also the pain, the suffering, the loss whatever the level or appearance. It is through the discovery of loss that we realize how much we loved, and that is a really good feeling, don't miss it!

Honoring the journey is one of my favorite parts of the process of connection because it reflects the life experience we create as we navigate life's journey. Personally, I have submerged myself in the stories of my life and have learned to re-write and edit along the way. If we can truly see our life as an honor, if we can truly embrace every moment good or bad and experience it to its fullest, we can experience a transformation. In my practice of this, it always leads to a place of surrendering, letting go of the painful thoughts that haunt me leaving me in a new, sometimes unfamiliar place, the new normal. Life was never intended to be perfect because we can't control it. In fact, when do we really learn the most? When things are going great or when there's a little challenge thrown in.

Healing the mind, body and spirit. Our daily experiences in living, loving, hurting and healing are so interconnected and happen so fast that we don't even notice or actively embrace our role in this power to heal ourselves. It is important to distinguish what I mean when I use the term healing, healing to me means to "become whole again," "complete." When our lives are disrupted, or compromised in any way we experience a change from an old normal to a new normal a "loss." Healing takes a conscious effort of realizing where we are, where we want to be and then developing a strategy to get there.

In the human condition stress takes an incredible toll on our mind, body, and soul. The stress hormones released into our systems are triggered every moment by our thoughts alone. If our thoughts go unregulated, we can very easily lose control. It can make us feel removed from what is happening around leaving us isolated and feeling alone. This happens all of the time in our daily life and is intensified when someone we love dies.

When we receive the news of a death, there is an instantaneous mental reaction of disbelief. It is our first reaction to loss. It has been called the "Unguarded Moment." You never know when it will come and rarely are you prepared for it. Even I, who is well versed and accustomed to receiving the information, when hearing the news for the first time will find myself speaking the words, "I don't believe it." It is human to experience shock when we hear the news, and shock takes its toll on us.

Some shock can take days or years to recover from. Imagine the news of your 19-year-old son being tragically killed in a late night car crash with friends. Imagine the sudden loss of your son taking his own life. Imagine hearing the most horrid news you can imagine. In that moment, and for many moments after, your brain and your body will just shut down. Like a computer on overload, it will crash and burn, it will cease to function as normal. It will happen to all of us.

Shock is there for a reason it will physically shut us down and it is important to realize our bodies need time to recover. It is good, normal, and important to experience shock for it forces us to absorb and recover. It is especially important to realize that you need time and you need to allow for that time. My advice to families when they have experienced a major shock event in their lives is to postpone any decisions regarding funeral plans. It is important to take all the time necessary to absorb and share the news with friends and family. You will find the brain working overtime to make an attempt to understand all of the details and process all of the stories related to the event. This can take many days. In some cases, information may not be

> *In that moment, and for many moments after, your brain and your body will just shut down. Like a computer on overload, it will crash and burn, it will cease to function as normal. It will happen to all of us.*

available, making it even harder to process because of shock. It is not possible to receive the value of the funeral journey when your brain is pre-occupied with a death event.

My advice to family and friends is to go and just be with them. Allow them to tell their story over and over even though there are no words that can be spoken to help. Bring food and drink. Sit with them and eat together. In this time of indescribable pain, it can and will be the only aspect of their life that connects them to this world. This is the time when they need that connection more than you can imagine. It is an opportunity to bring some sense of normalcy to an upside down world.

The second reaction after hearing the news of a death is the need to share it with someone. There is a need to share with others, to process and confirm the information. After receiving the information, I will typically reach out to my wife Nancy and tell her or anyone else who might be around. The need to share attends to the brain's need to qualify and process the data, and to verify our reality. It will appear in emails, Facebook, Twitter, and all of the social media possibly moments after the event. In accident cases, some families report hearing about it on social media even before the call from other family members or the police. The need for a family to tell the story is as old as time itself, and has some very significant healing affects.

It is important to realize that we all need to tell our story and I encourage all of you to ask, but be prepared for an answer you may find challenging. My first experience with this was when my dad's close friend died. It was one of my first experiences transferring someone from a home where they had died. We had just entered the house and, since I knew the spouse, I greeted her with the typical "Hi, how are you?" Well, her answer was, "Terrible, my husband just died." Needless to say, I do not ask that question unless I am ready to really hear an answer!

Recently I worked with a family who lost a parent in a skiing accident where one of the family members was present at the scene. My experience with any accident or traumatic death is that you will frequently find family members who feel in some way responsible or at least question their part in it. During arrangements two days later (remember shock needs some time), I asked the family member who had been with him to tell me exactly what happened. It was a very difficult experience for all of us there to hear him share every detail, but one of great importance.

> *When we experience a traumatic death our brains will continue to play that movie over and over again in our head until it is played out or we just can't do it anymore. The exercise of telling the story helps bring clarity and healing*

After he concluded his remarks, we were all aware of just how difficult it was for him and how he blamed himself for not doing more. It was also the first time that the family had heard every detail of how things had happened. I recommended that he continue to tell the story, knowing full well that when we experience a traumatic death our brains will continue to play that movie over and over again in our head until it is played out or we just can't do it anymore. The exercise of telling the story helps bring clarity and healing, and he was very brave to do this. I know that in time, he will see his struggle diminish and he will find a place of healing. The healing will come, in part because he was asked to tell the story and also because of his courage to tell the story.

Many other examples come to mind with family members wondering if they had done this or done that, it might have changed the outcome. It is my hope for all of them that they have found peace and healing. The day my dad died, my stepmother asked me if I thought that my father might have lived if she had called for an ambulance earlier. I told her she had done the best she could do in the moment and that is all one can ask.

I remember attending a seminar on suicide presented by a woman whose son had committed suicide at the age of twenty-two. He had left no note, which complicated her grief and left her asking, "Why?"

I had always wondered how long is appropriate to question why.

After the seminar, I asked her how long she had spent asking the question. Her answer to me was,

"Until I couldn't do it anymore." In life we will go whatever distance we need to go. I have found the human spirit can handle almost anything when given a challenge. How we do it, how we get there is a choice we make. At some point, this mother had made the decision to move past the question and allowed herself the time to grieve and heal. For this mother's situation, sometimes there are no apparent answers; but in the giving up, or letting go, we can move forward to a place of healing and peace.

The third reaction, or need, is to visually confirm the data. Once again, the brain and its infinite desire to figure everything out will want to see the evidence. There is a very strong fear or concern to experience this. If you are in active grief and especially if it has been a sudden or unexpected death you will find a stronger need for this. I constantly find myself explaining to families that this idea of confirmation has nothing to do with remembering someone, because many people say they want to remember them the way they were.

When my dad died, I was physically involved in CPR and present in his house throughout the whole process. I have also seen many people who have died, and when I first saw him I knew exactly what I was looking at. My need for confirmation was immediately met, but I am not the norm. I have had families choose to view whatever was appropriate or possible to see, perhaps a hand or a foot that might not have been traumatized in an accident. I have also had families choose to see the person's body intact even though there might be significant trauma and it may be unpleasant. In many instances the actual visual experience may be much, much better than what the imagination had created beforehand. In one particular instance I took a picture of a tattoo to provide the necessary confirmation that the body was indeed that of their loved one. Our role in our service is to lead them down the path no matter what the path looks like, preparing the way and preparing them for what they will be experiencing.

That path can be difficult, but it has been confirmed by generations that having the body present at the services is paramount to one's healing experience.

Most people think that seeing someone dead is

bad. Although it may be difficult, I'm here to tell you that it is necessary. It confirms the reality and it provides the data, the necessary facts, to the brain. When my birth mother died in Baltimore, I had the good fortune of being present, which is not always possible. I was outside of her room near the nurse's station when her husband and my sister came running from her room. Both my mother's husband and my sister work in the medical field and because their lives are devoted to extending life, they both struggle with the concept of death. It is not uncommon to feel fear, anxiety, panic, and loss of breath as well as other physical reactions when we see someone that has died.

My work experience puts me in another stratosphere, so what I saw when I entered her room was an angel. I saw my mother free of pain and suffering, and I want to believe I saw joy in her face. To me, she looked like she had lost twenty years in age, her skin looked silky white and smooth, and her expression appeared peaceful in a way I had never seen before. In life, she had weathered many years of struggle and discomfort, but now she seemed at peace. She looked released from her pain, her body now only the shell that in life had concealed a purity and beauty never before seen. I'm glad I was able to be there, I hope you, too, have that opportunity with a loved one. I also know that the death event comes in many different colors and flavors. It is not always what I experienced with my mother, and it can be extremely difficult. What I want to share with you is that we cannot escape it, for it will come to all of us and it is our responsibility to prepare for it.

When people say that they want to remember their loved one "as they were," they may be using this as a way to avoid this reality. If you don't hear anything else, hear this: I'm here to tell you that seeing someone dead has nothing to do with remembering them in life. Seeing someone dead has everything to do with seeing someone dead; it confirms the reality that the person who has died is no longer a part of our physical world. Your life as you know it has changed and it will not be the same again. If we do this properly we will be experiencing the hole that this loss has created, and then we can fill it with all of the memories we have and share and love. We need to process this as part of our journey forward in our personal health.

Seeing someone they love without their life force present in the physical body will cause people to have an emotional reaction. It will undoubtedly feel uncomfortable and painful in some way. This reaction can, in fact, be the most important reaction one can have. To be allowed to exhaust the emotional impact of this event may well be the healthiest thing you can do. This pain may go on for days, weeks, and possibly years if not exhausted correctly.

I often tell the story of the internal combustion engine as it relates to emotion and the experience of grieving. If you were to take a rag and stuff it up the exhaust pipe of your car, over time the car's engine would overheat causing it to breakdown. This is also what happens to the human engine. The heart will break down if we do not allow our system to exhaust the feelings and experience the grieving process. The traditional funeral event has been in existence since time began and it has provided the opportunity for "exhausting." I have heard many suggest that the traditional funeral event is barbaric. My response to those comments "It is not barbaric, it is ancient." It is ancient because, since the beginning of time, those that are left after death have participated in the mourning process while carrying their deceased loved ones to their grave thus experiencing the journey towards healing. I refer to it as bearing the burden of grief.

Recently, in the United States and Canada there has been a movement to remove the body from the funeral service. Families are choosing to have a service without evidence of the death present. Research is limited but initial findings show those who grieve without a physical connection with the body experience more long term issues with their grief. The absence of the body complicates our grieving process because the brain has nothing to use as evidence of the loss, therefore leaving the mind to perpetually research the dilemma causing pathological results. It should be noted that the United States and Canada are the only places in the world today that have removed the body from funeral services since the beginning of time.

We all probably know someone who has died from

a broken heart not long after losing their spouse. I can think of many and sometimes it happens merely days after their spouse's death.

Now picture yourself in this position: Your spouse of fifty years has just died suddenly, leaving you in a place you have never been in before and one that many of us do not plan adequately for. The mere thought of this is fraught with confusion, anxiety, and fear. You are momentarily paralyzed, caught up in the shock and unable to process simple thoughts. Your first thought might be to call one of your children or a close family member for help and advice. The conversation usually begins with, "Dad just died. What should I do?" The first response would typically be, "Whatever you think, Mom!" The conversation would continue, "I don't know, we never talked about it." Then, "Well, did he want to be cremated or buried?" The answer would be something like, "I don't know. What should we do?" Finally, someone says, "Whatever you think, Mom."

In most cases, there is uneasiness about having a dead body in the family. Even naming the funeral home will be hard to do because often we either can't remember the name or haven't had a recent experience with one. As a reaction to loss, and while experiencing the shock of death, most families will call the funeral home where they last attended a funeral. In fact, they will remember what the building looked like, and maybe even its location, before remembering the name. They may not even remember whether it was a good or a bad experience. This is not uncommon; it is because of the shock and the stress hormones' numbing the impact on our brains. Often when I receive the first call from a family, they will begin with, "Hello, this is..." and then, "My dad died and we want cremation or a burial."

Obviously, the first major concern when someone dies is deciding what to do with the body. When I first started in the funeral profession, there was no need for this concern as there was a traditional way. For Christians, there were two days of calling followed by a service in the church or the funeral home and a burial in a cemetery. Other cultures had their significant rituals, but they were consistent with tradition. Although there have been significant changes in the US and Canada over the past fifty years, I believe we are trending down a path of great concern. To combat this, we must accept that death is a fact of life and embrace the event as a healing and beneficial journey. The first question and concern should be, "What should we do to help those we love that have been affected by the loss in their life?" Secondly, "How will we transition to a place of 'new normal' without the deceased?"

The baby boomer generation has been at the forefront of recent change in the funeral profession. It is understandable in many ways because it is the baby boomer culture currently making the funeral decisions for their loved ones. If we can't show them the value in a product or service and they don't have a previous experience to draw from, they won't purchase it. In general, the funeral service industry has "dropped the ball" in our efforts to challenge and guide the public in their struggle toward what we know to be the healing and valuable experience of a funeral. Often the discussion will revolve around what so-and-so did that they liked, or "we really never talked about it," or "dad didn't want any fuss," etc. There is very little conversation related to what we are feeling, or what to do to help in the healing for those who may need some help.

In over forty years in the funeral profession, I have worked with thousands of families and have personal losses of my own. The "average" family experiences a death in their family every seven years or so and many family members may never be involved in any of the funeral planning. Without experience, how can they know what is best for them? What experience, or knowledge, do they have to draw on? We in the funeral profession may have as little as two to three hours to meet and discuss many highly emotional and important elements with the family as we help them formulate the funeral plan. It is extremely difficult to cram years of knowledge into that short time. The difficulty in getting the information to the family members present at that meeting is compounded by the physical shock, emotional stress and struggle some families experience.

My best advice for families is to extensively research the complex issues surrounding grief. There are many good books available today and the internet has become a helpful tool. Once we begin to understand how the human body and brain work under this stress, we can better understand the direction we must take. From a very simplistic view, we must embrace the actual death event in order to receive the ability to understand the true meaning of the loss in our lives. It is hard and exhausting work, but it is work that has significant value and connects all of us in our human existence.

Dr. Alan Wolfelt, a leader in the study of thanatology (the study of death), writes:

> *"Grief and mourning are about the capacity to experience change and movement; to reach the other side by going through, rather than around; by not avoiding but by understanding and accepting that grief and mourning are who you are and that it is not only acceptable but therapeutic to cry and to commemorate our loss through rituals."*[2]

2 See more at: http://www.centerforloss.com

Chapter Eight

Kids

"One touch of nature makes the whole world kin."
—*William Shakespeare*

O ften in our business, well-intentioned parents make personal decisions for their children and grandchildren, believing a very instinctive thought: "If I can remove the problem, they will not have to hurt."

As a parent, we all have written within our DNA the program of protecting our children from danger and the experience of pain in their lives. When we are threatened with bodily harm or illness, or when we experience any challenge from life, we kick into the protector mode so as to protect our children from experiencing harm, a basic survival instinct.

When there is the emotional trauma of death in the family, oftentimes well-intentioned parents and grandparents will make decisions eliminating the need of having them present in the planning and funeral services. They will create real time excuses to keep them from attending any experiences or at least limiting their exposure.

I believe this to be an instinctive reaction and if not processed correctly, it can be harmful to a child's growth and development. I say this because as a life lesson and a teaching moment, the reality is everyone they know and love will someday die. What will best serve them will be to offer supportive teaching and loving guidance throughout the experience.

When my daughter was five years old and in her first year of school, a sparrow built a nest between the window and the triple track storm window frame in her bedroom. We watched as the sparrow laid her eggs and for many weeks we anxiously awaited the birth of the baby birds. Every day at noon when Lauren arrived home from school, she would run upstairs to see if the miracle had occurred. One morning while she was at school it finally happened.

Four baby sparrows graced her windowsill to our complete excitement and joy.

A few days later, I received a frantic call from my wife saying that the baby birds were dead. Apparently the mother had abandoned the nest because of all the distraction we had caused. Our daughter was due to arrive home on the noon bus at any moment and I was given instructions to do something before she arrived. In the panic of the moment I transformed into super dad the protector, I swooped in without a conscious thought to save the day, or so I thought. I had apparently decided the best way to protect and serve was by dispensing of the dead baby birds in a way you might consider for dead goldfish.

I am not proud of this moment but I love sharing it, as my intention was to save my daughter from hurt and pain. In that moment, I was totally disconnected. Both my brain and my heart were in full protect mode (a form of shock). In reflection, you would think that someone who deals with death everyday as I do would have known better. The truth is, it's not so easy. Old patterns, thoughts and instincts come into play, and we make mistakes.

Once I realized my error, which obviously came moments after my daughter's return from school, I kicked into funeral director mode. I suggested we find a surrogate bird to commemorate and bury at a later time. Fortunately, this seemed to do the trick because Lauren immediately began preparing the guest list of neighborhood children to invite and determined a day and time for the burial service.

When the day arrived, it was a grey and rainy Saturday morning. After the seemingly more important decisions of what outfit to wear for the services, we set up chairs with the surrogate bird (an adult Robin I had found in the backyard) placed in an appropriate box on a table in our garage. I had prepared some age appropriate words to share on death and dying and the guests began to arrive right on schedule. It was "go time" and I was ready to deliver my best work. Halfway into the first paragraph, my daughter interrupted me with "When are we going to bury the bird?" directing me to promptly prepare the hole so as to complete the burial.

The service was over. My hope of delivering the gift of life-affirming, comforting words to everyone present, was crushed, superseded by an instinctive need to complete the burial. We did so and the service was ended, no food was served. That one simple experience proved to me just how powerful the activity of a ritual burial is and why it's so important to us.

Someone once said, "When words are inadequate, have a ritual." Rituals help us to experience and express our deepest thoughts and feelings about the great events of our life. The funeral ritual has always been a public tradition that enables us to experience and express our faith, as well as our beliefs and feelings about a loved one who has encountered death.

I tell the story of the five-year-old constantly pulling at his mother's dress as the minister conducted prayers over the casket and open grave. After the prayers were concluded, the minister came over to talk to the mother and the little boy. He asked the boy what the fussing was about. Without any hesitation, he walked over to the hole in the ground and pointed down into the grave at the grave box ready to receive his grandmother's casket and asked, "Is that Heaven?" Out of the mouths of babes come the most amazing things.

I recall the evening we had to tell our five-year-old son that his Nana died. His response as he sat there in reflection of this information was, "Well, I guess that's the end of her." We laughed and it was good. He loved her very much, but he hadn't had the many years we had had to establish a relationship with her. His five-year-old mind processed very clearly the information conveyed, it was simple to him.

I tell parents over and over, our grief is directly proportionate to the number of years we had shared in a relationship. Although it may have been a special relationship, a five-year-old does not have the emotional or the time investment in the relationship that we do and therefore, one should not expect too much struggle. In my advice to parents I suggest they deal with children at the child's level, telling them as little as needed and only answering the questions they ask. They will ask more later if needed. Perhaps the most helpful thought I can offer is, as their parent, they are most concerned about you. Your reactions and non-reactions will be their barometer to how they react and behave. You are the focus in their lives when stress and struggle appear. If you are struggling, all they need is some assurance and honesty, and they will respond appropriately.

There is much information out there about the developmental stages of children and their response to loss, and most of this information is very good. Just remember you are the one they want to see healthy, happy and safe. If you do the work necessary for your healing, they will be fine.

Chapter Nine

Burial

*"Shall I not have intelligence with the earth? Am
I not partly leaves and vegetable mould myself"*
—Henry David Thoreau

Whether we're five or fifty, there is nothing as powerful as a plain old burial. While many people are eliminating experiencing the actual burial from the funeral ritual these days, the journey from the church or funeral home to the grave is as old as time itself. I call this journey, "bearing the burden of grief."

Cremation hasn't helped things as it makes it easier to put off decisions or even eliminate a burial. It is amazing just how many families we serve who, because of cremation, do not finalize any burial plans or final resting place for their cremated remains.

I have many concerns for families because of this. I have witnessed both prolonged and pathological grief reactions as a result of the decision to either not have services or not complete the process of burial. I have seen cremains gather dust in our funeral home and in the closets of friends. I have seen families scatter cremated remains in favorite places around the country, leaving them no specific place to commemorate the life of the individual. I believe we all need to feel that our life meant something, that our life had significance. Although scattering our cremated remains on top of a favorite mountain or in a favorite body of water sounds comforting and could meet some needs of significance, it provides no permanent memorial or evidence of one's life.

Philosophically, I believe that we as a culture have transitioned to a place of disconnect. Our communications have become less connected and personal. We don't gather as families did in the past, and we don't make time in our schedules to maintain family and social relationships in person like we used to. Whether we realize it or not this disconnect has gradually put us out in the world alone, not feeling the strong relational connections we once had. Why should, then, we be concerned with getting together to bury our loved one?

Throughout history, the local cemetery has provided the historical evidence of our heritage. Today, because of the increase in cremation, our culture is eliminating the immediate need for burial and gradually eliminating the burial altogether. This cultural shift taking place today is very concerning to me. It is my feeling that we need more connection, not less!

A great example of the powerful connection of family is what we consistently witness at graveside ceremonies. I have witnessed families scattered throughout the cemetery, discovering deceased family members from generations past. I continually witness numerous stories and memories shared as families introduce their children to their ancestors for the first time in their lives. Because the grave is such an incredible reminder of our heritage, it helps connect us to our history. It brings relevance and meaning to who we are, where came from, and what were made of.

I ask the question, "Who are we and where did we come from?" Is that a question we can readily answer? How much time do we spend sharing the family stories and the history of our families? Throughout history, the local cemetery has provided the evidence of that history and heritage.

As an example of my heritage and its significance, if I ever start to feel sorry for myself because I'm overworked or stressed, all I need to do is go to the cemetery where my grandfather and grandmother are buried. If after a few minutes I'm not over it, there is something really wrong. You see, I come from a family that worked very hard and gave up much to get through the Great Depression. I can only imagine how difficult that must have been. I never in my life heard them complain or whine about how hard, or how unfair it was. These are the people from whom and where I came and they are what I'm made of. When I stand there at their grave or bring them back into my thoughts, I am re-connected with their resolve and strength; I am strong, I can overcome this.

Recently I purchased a number of graves in a local cemetery, providing a memorial and a final resting place for myself as well as the next few generations of my family. My hope is to purchase a large monument or grave marker to put the name "Anthony" on in large block letters. This marker will be there forever and will provide an ever-present reminder of our family's presence on this earth. I am not doing it to shout out how important I am, but to shout out how important my family is to me.

> *"You have come into a hard world. I know of only one easy place in it, and that is the grave."*
>
> —*Henry Ward Beecher*

One day as I was waiting for a family in a local cemetery, I began to question the purpose of the many different grave markers on the grounds. There were big ones and small ones, square ones and round ones. I couldn't understand what was so important about their differences. Later that year, I was working a visitation at the funeral home and having a conversation with the secretary from one of our local churches. She was sharing with me the experience of purchasing a new grave marker in the very cemetery where I had recently questioned their significance. I asked her why she picked out the rose granite tower marker she had so proudly described to me. With an irreverent, almost disgusted look she turned to me and said, "So we can find the grave." I was being schooled in the importance of the differences.

Many amazing things have happened at graves. The grave can be one of the most significant places and experiences on earth. It brings closure and reality to life as we return our mortal remains to that which is bound by earthly laws, for we cannot take our bodies with us. They are and will always be a reflection of this life in this world, and they stay here.

The veteran's ceremony is designed to take place at the grave of a veteran and can be very moving, touching and powerful. For those who have not experienced it, there is a very significant message conveyed. It is a message of thanksgiving for the person's commitment to his country in whatever capacity they served. It is, in fact, a high honor to acknowledge their service, and those who preside over the grave during this ceremony know this. I have attended many; to this day I am still personally moved by its impact.

At my brother-in-law's services for his mom in Baltimore, he brought six shovels to the grave so that all of us attending could assist in the burial. After the prayers, we had the casket lowered into the grave box, the grave box lid placed, and shovels were passed out to all who wished to participate. Each one of us, one by one took shovels full of dirt and filled in the grave. It took us the next twenty to thirty minutes to complete the burial. Up until this moment I had never witnessed a family completing the burial like that.

Typically, my experience had been that after the family leaves the grave, our staff and the cemetery staff completes the burial. What I experienced after we had completed moving all the earth into the grave and packing it down was a sense of completion, a sense of satisfaction, and it felt good.

I think everyone should have the option to perform the actual burial themselves

Living and Dying

Chapter Ten

Feelings

*"The earth is rude, silent, incomprehensible at first;
be not discouraged - keep on - there are divine
things, well enveloped; I swear to you there are
divine things more beautiful than words can tell."*
—Walt Whitman

I have recently surrendered and embraced the thought or concept of communication as an emotional experience. For years I had tried to keep emotion out by trying to operate exclusively from my mind and not allowing my heart to participate. My mind was strong and I had developed it to work rather well. What I have re-learned is that when we live from a place of intellect, we become disconnected from our heart and with how it feels. If we disconnect with how it feels, we miss the opportunity to heal. And, if we don't heal we stay wounded, or less than whole.

Feeling is a key to our life and the barometer of our connection between head and heart. When someone we care about has died, we are going to experience a thought and an associated feeling about it. If we do not, we need to take a close look at that because we cannot run or hide from it, it is a part of our nature. For some of us, we would rather find a way to escape this nightmare.

In my relationship with my partner (cousin), I had to lead from my heart and reconnect with how it felt to be a member of his family as opposed to his business partner in order to experience healing. The journey toward healing involved choosing a path based on feeling but started with a conscious thought to change and journey from the heart. We get to make the choice, to choose. We all have the choice, and truthfully all we need is to be "willing." If we're willing to make the effort, there will be growth and there will be healing. I encourage you to make the choice of living and loving through all of life's ups and downs, there is no better ride.

Many years ago, I had the experience of working with a doctor who had just lost his beautiful young twenty-year-old daughter to cancer. The experience entering into their family residence to transfer the young woman into our care was one of the few times in my life that I was actually scared for my well-being. After arriving at their home, I witnessed a range of emotion that went from hysteria to anger, to being totally incapacitated by emotion. It was not an experience I had ever witnessed before that day. Although it was an experience of intense feeling, there was a very pathological flavor to it. There was a sense of madness in the air, total, uncontrollable madness. My only way to make sense of it was, being a doctor and being committed to keeping people alive and yet not being able to keep your own daughter alive, can drive you mad. I have never experienced anything like this since, but it would suffice to say the doctor's willingness to feel and heal from his loss was never completed. There were no services for this beautiful girl of such a young age and his death followed in two years.

Struggling with feelings is serious work and one that requires life affirming and supportive experiences that allow us to express, exhaust and feel out loud, with the support and care from our family, friends and community. Without this sense of community support, grief can overwhelm us and in some cases kill.

Another experience I had was with a friend's daughter who died of cancer. She was also in her twenties. The death event experienced here was far different from the previous story because the emotions and feelings were being expressed in a very open, understanding, supportive, honest and loving manner. Her death was on the second floor of an old house with a difficult staircase, and we needed to use our body transfer pouch to negotiate the stairs. After some frank discussion, it was revealed that the idea of bringing her down the stairs in that manner did not feel good or right to them. They had been caring for her for many months—comforting her, bathing her, whatever the need. They had all grown comfortable together with their feelings and her inevitable death. It was determined that the fiancé, stepdad, and I would carry her down stairs in our arms and then place her on our cot to transfer her the rest of the way to our vehicle. I explained the issues we confronted as we proceeded and it went perfectly for them.

Their connection and ability to express their needs and feelings were well thought out and honest. It was obvious they had done their feeling and healing work to prepare for this and we were there to assist them in their journey. There were calling hours and services honoring her life. Being connected to thoughts and feelings worked for them, and they were well on their way in their journey of healing. Their journey continues.

Chapter Eleven

Healing

"Now I see the secret of the making of the best persons. It is to grow in the open air, and to eat and sleep with the earth."
—Walt Whitman

I have so many stories to share regarding living a healthy life because of my experience in the funeral business. Having to wake up every day and enter a world of loss has been a great gift to me. No day is the same and all I have to do is care about people. We should all have such a job!

People often joke how my job is recession proof or not affected by the economy. The saying "the only thing certain is death and taxes" comes to mind. You might be surprised that in the last forty years there have been significant and consistent changes. Probably one of the biggest differences or changes in the past few years is how important logistics has become. Years ago we did not have such a mobile society. People were born, raised and died in the same communities. Our children today are living, visiting and studying in other countries. We have families living apart while spouses travel to distant cities for work and then return on weekends for family time. Commerce is conducted on the internet—Skype and web casting are the new norms, to name just a few.

One interesting story where scheduling and logistics comes to mind is the death of one woman's husband. In the arrangement process when it came time to schedule the funeral, I was told we needed to wait five weeks for the service as she was scheduled to leave for a cruise. Although this story is a rare occurrence, there are more and more families trying to work around scheduled plans and events. Most important to remember is "death is not convenient" and we need to accept the fact that sometimes we must be willing to change our plans to accommodate it. Being one of life's most significant events you might think we would take notice and stop the world for a few days or weeks.

Today as a funeral director, not only do I need to care, but I am often called upon to help coordinate scheduling and travel plans, and to help facilitate payment plans. I coordinate and staff gatherings at funeral homes, personal homes, and country clubs. I plan, and in some cases provide food service for receptions. I order flowers, prepare newspaper notices, and I also provide web-based connections to Facebook through our websites and other social media. We offer videotape services. At times I even preside over a service or graveside. If you can think of it, we do it. Then I make it all happen seamlessly and flawlessly in a matter of a couple of days. We also provide resource materials and speaking programs for our community. We offer before death pre-arrangement opportunities, and after death support services.

What other profession does this? While wedding or event planners may have the most similar job description, they have months, if not years, to accomplish these things. We have days. The fact we are dealing with someone's death can be a very anxious and difficult time for most people and it puts additional stress on our work. If you are ever going to witness distress, fighting, dysfunction, and irrational behavior within a family, you are going to see it here. Being a moderator, coach, editor and guide is an everyday role that we perform as funeral directors.

It should be noted that in the midst of loss, our interpersonal skills and emotional connections in the heat of the moment, can be strained, short-circuiting our common sense. It is of paramount importance that we maintain our center, our connection with self. It should also be noted that in order to help facilitate and moderate a family crisis, it takes a highly trained, committed, and caring team of support staff, for one cannot do this alone.

Perhaps one of the most important elements the funeral professional brings to a grieving family's world at the time of a death is "normalcy." I live in a world where I am constantly reminded that we all die. In fact, I get that call every day. When it is your turn to call, you need that personal and emotional connection with normalcy. You need someone who has been there to listen and advise you as you navigate a journey you've possibly never experienced. You need someone who is comfortable with the death experience that brings a strong presence and calm to an otherwise anxious and often unfamiliar time. You need someone who has asked themselves the hard questions, and who sees death as a normal part of life.

What I mean by that is that with life comes death; it is a normal evolution of what happens to us. We have no control over the length of time we're here, and we need to realize that there will come a time when what we know to be true today will be different tomorrow.

When that moment comes, you need us because we all need to feel safe, loved, and cared for. We need someone that can help coordinate the simpler daily activities you will be struggling with, someone who can help with logistics and scheduling. We need someone who has experience and knows what works and what does not work, and can communicate that. We need someone we can trust, a trusted guide, someone who sincerely wants your family to experience a journey of healing, and we need someone who cares and wants to be there. When dealing with loss, there is an element of discomfort.

I see our role as one of responsibility first and empathy second. What I mean by that is that it is my responsibility to share with you my knowledge in the healing journey before you, and to help you craft an experience to your individual needs. I can only hope you don't deny your feelings or abuse your connections with family and community. In addition to everything else I have mentioned here, it's incumbent on me to be a good communicator and counselor. I need to be able to walk you down a path where you feel safe and secure, and I need to set that stage in a few hours.

The old way of funeral directing has changed. We are being called to perform superhuman functions in a time of distress and questioning. We are being required to develop new paradigms as the old ones no longer work. We are a profession reinventing itself, re-connecting to a new normal. Not an enviable task but one demanded of us. Those who are successful will remain in this time honored profession. Those who do not will be gone.

The father of one of my son's good friends died in Europe recently. They called us looking for our counsel as they were struggling with the funeral home assisting them. They reached out to my son to connect with us for some guidance. Nancy and I were actually driving home from a friend's home in Little Rock, Arkansas when I finally reached them in Germany.

It was apparent that they had experienced an unwilling and perhaps unqualified funeral professional. In addition to the death being unexpected, the funeral home did very little to assist in the family's needs. After twenty minutes of discussion I had offered many different thoughts and suggestions, the most important being that if you are not satisfied with your funeral professional, go get another one. There are many good and qualified professionals out there, but there are also a few not as qualified. Don't settle for okay.

The funeral experience you have and create is a onetime opportunity. You do not get a second chance.

One of the biggest obstacles we have in funeral service is the idea that we are going to take advantage of your grief and then "sell" you things you don't need. Sometimes it may feel like selling because of our knowledge regarding the importance of the funeral ritual, and our struggle to communicate that importance at a highly emotional time. It is important that we understand that death puts us in a state of shock, disconnect or anxiousness, and we can become fearful in our vulnerability.

> *Don't settle for okay.*
> *The funeral experience you have and create is a onetime opportunity.*
> *You do not get a second chance.*

It is also important to realize that this transaction is one that is impractical, much like a wedding. As a parent I know it would have been much more practical to have had our daughter elope. Instead we all chose the more impractical, more costly path and as a result we have a lot of great memories from the experience to cherish. Although the general consensus is that the wedding experience should be more fun in many ways, I can honestly say that my dad's funeral was one of the most amazing experiences in my life. Not only was it memorable with many good feelings, it was also very meaningful because I had chosen every word and every song that was included in the service. The more we are willing to participate, the greater the value.

> *The more we are willing to participate, the greater the value.*

As a baby boomer, I know that in order for me to do or purchase anything, you are going to have to show me the value. "Value vs. Price" is the new model, and the experience is a key factor. In the world today, this value vs. price model is everywhere, evident by the success of internet marketing and discount stores, airlines, etc. In funeral service we have an experience that one would rather not have to do or pay for at all—a death.

I have a stereo system that costs more than what some people want to pay for a funeral experience. In fact, many years ago, I once said that to a family member who was complaining about the cost of our service—not a good move by the way—but my point is that it's all relative. What we are willing to pay for has to have value, and in my case the money I spent on my stereo system was spent on something I knew would provide me years of value in my experience of listening to music. In his case, the money I was asking him to pay represented an experience not wanted of which he had no reference of the value.

Due to the fact that we expect funerals will hurt emotionally or be unpleasant, we may choose to avoid or minimize the experience. We may also minimize the experience because of family issues, financial issues and a variety of other concerns.

We have had over sixty years of experience in our community observing families in their time of grief. What we have experienced time and time again are the positive effects of affirming their feelings as they navigate their loss. In my experience, it actually is life affirming, rewarding and inspiring to guide those down that path to healing.

So, if you can, picture yourself in this place. You know you need to do something but you want to minimize your pain and simplify an experience that you are not familiar with. You may be afraid and feeling totally out of control. Then, to top it off, I am there to ask you to pay a considerably large amount of money for this privilege. How am I going to get through to you the value vs. price model? It is my job on a daily basis to suggest that you do something that may be difficult and potentially painful. You're hurting, unstable, and then I work to sell you things you don't want to buy. It's not an enviable position. You would be much more agreeable spending lots of money on a wedding, a nice car, or a great stereo system in my case.

Although it may not be an enviable position, it is our mission, passion and commitment to our community to assist families in their journey through grief. Our goal, or final outcome, is to have all those that we serve say, "We're glad we did this," whatever their decisions might be. We believe that everyone is entitled to a life affirming experience that will connect us to our heritage, community and life's significance while at the same time using appropriate symbols and meeting their financial concerns. While this journey may be affected by many things, if we remain open and willing there is always a way, a path towards healing. On a purely financial level, there are many options that allow all family's financial needs and concerns to be met. We are highly skilled at helping families find their road to healing no matter what the obstacles. Just ask.

Chapter Twelve

Undertaking

"Your deepest roots are in nature. No matter whom you are, where you live, or what kind of life you lead, you remain irrevocably linked with the rest of creation."
—Charles Cook

We've already discussed the hearing, sharing and seeing components of the death event; now let's discuss the gathering, connection, reflection and celebrating components.

The gathering—this can be either informal or formal. The power of community and the support it offers is one of great comfort. It lets us know we are not alone, that there are friends and family that care about and love us.

You see, since the beginning of time we have gathered as community and honored the dead. We have been doing it one way for so long that it amazes me that we think we need to change it, because it obviously works.

Recently we were commemorating the fiftieth anniversary of John F. Kennedy's assassination. There have been specials on television and interviews with FBI agents and personal assistants. The people there that day retell their stories as if it had happened

Everett Collection Inc / Alamy Stock Photo by Stan Stearns, Photographer

just the other day. For those of us who experienced the shock and remember that day, we can most likely tell you where we were and possibly even what we were wearing when the news came to us. The days following, we all experienced the drama unfold as

Lee Harvey Oswald was exposed and killed. Then there was the funeral. Millions of people around the

Photos above and below by Abbie Rowe, 1905-1967, Photographer (NARA record: 8451352) [Public domain], via Wikimedia Commons

world gathered around their TV sets and wept as we witnessed both the funeral and the caisson parade to the cemetery. The now infamous images of a family torn apart by grief are part of our culture. We gathered as a world community in our grief, we wept both with our families and with strangers on the street. We experienced the power of gathering and most people, if asked, would say they needed it.

We have experienced the funerals of other heads of state, Popes, pop stars, etc., and feel the need to participate in some way. We also have experienced the lack of opportunity to gather as a community, as we did when Andy Griffith died. Many of us grew up with Andy of Mayberry and when he died recently there were no services, thereby denying us of the opportunity to share the loss of someone we grew up with.

The attack on the World Trade Center is another powerful example of our need for connection. I remember the morning of September 11th vividly. In that moment, I experienced all of the human needs of connection: hearing, seeing, and sharing. When I first heard about it, I immediately turned on the television to see what was happening. I then called my closest loved ones to share the news and to find out if they were okay. I'm sure that you, too, experienced these same natural reactions to this event.

Our funeral home was called upon to serve one of the victims of this attack. I once again witnessed the powerful need for gathering, connection, reflection and celebration. In this case there were multiple gatherings, one in the moment and one a year later when the remains were identified and returned to the family. There were also many group gatherings at the site of the attack. There was a significant experience of connection. Many people who never knew this man were moved by the mere intensity of the event to connect with the family. People that had never known him personally felt compelled to reach out to both each other and the victim's family.

Reflection still continues to this day as we mourn the loss of life and liberty while we experience the many other effects of the terror attack. Monuments have been erected, dollars collected for the victims' families, and the acknowledgment of our public service professionals continues. The experience of this magnitude took many years to resolve, and for some it still continues to be a struggle.

As I mentioned earlier, my dad's funeral gathering was one of the most powerful experiences in my life. Being an expert in this field, I had created an experience where all of my human needs were provided for. My dad was in the most expensive casket I could buy because it made me feel good as his son to do so. I feel that it is important to share with you my thoughts regarding this casket decision. My dad always wanted the best of everything but couldn't always afford it, so it made me feel "good" to be able to do this for him, not a rational decision. In contrast, when my grandmother died we choose a moderately priced casket because of the way she lived her life, modestly. This is typically the manner in which families choose funeral products, as a reflection of how their loved one lived their lives or how it makes them feel.

By having my dad's body in a casket at the gathering, we addressed the need (both mental and emotional) for those who cared about him to experience his death and say goodbye. You have probably heard the sentiments such as, "You would not have a baptism without the baby." Or, "You would not have a wedding without the bride and groom." In this way of thinking, how can we begin to truly celebrate a life until we have had the experience of the death and reflected on its meaning to us?

Yes, death is difficult to process. It makes us cry and feel sad. Death makes us feel things we don't like. Or, maybe more accurately, it makes us feel things we aren't comfortable feeling.

The human brain is an amazing tool. Its primary function is to protect us, figure things out and file the data learned. Without the proper evidence (the body), it can be made to work overtime in this endeavor (you've experienced your imagination), and cause distress and in some cases pathological symptoms. As an example of how the brain, or imagination, can play with you, one day a few months after my dad's death, I saw his old handicapped van (which had been sold) driving down the highway. Even though I had been very involved in his death at the time and his body present, making it very real, I drove as fast as I could to catch up with the van to see who was driving it. My guess is that it was not pathological because I can remember laughing at myself. It is good to laugh at yourself sometimes.

The simple concept of experiencing the exercise of saying goodbye should not be undervalued. It is the simple act of seeing the body that confirms the reality that we will never be able to see this person again, at least in our lifetime. Our world as we know it has changed; it will never be the same, the old normal. Doing this is difficult but it can be and is designed to be an opportunity for us to experience saying goodbye. In the process of saying goodbye there may be many other things that may have gone unspoken in the relationship. I see it as an exercise in finalizing unfinished business so that one can get on with, or move forward in life, the new normal.

It is like the opening up and cleaning of a wound so that it will heal properly.

I have seen and heard many individuals process and heal from dysfunction by merely having a conversation with their dead loved one. They have in this final exercise cleared the trash from their trash basket on their hard drive clearing the way for healing. I encourage everyone to consider dealing with unfinished business at this time. It is like the opening up and cleaning of a wound so that it will heal properly. It is very simply a basic truth that unresolved issues in one's life can cause illness and can even kill—I have seen it happen.

One young teenager that had lost her dad couldn't make her way into the room with her father's casket. After the public calling hours, I approached her and asked if she wanted to go in with me to see her dad. She accepted my offer and we entered the room that she had avoided all afternoon. It was as if there was an explosion when she yelled out, "That's not my father!" She went running from the building.

Another family I served pulled me aside prior to the commencement of calling hours to tell me that their family members were saying that it was not their father. I ran to the office in a panic wondering if we had placed the wrong body in the casket. (I'm sure it's happened before, just not at our firm.) My staff assured me we had not.

Although these are not the normal reactions from

families, what it does point out is that both events revealed a truth in a difficult way. The truth is that the dead body we are seeing really isn't our loved one. I, of course, felt terrible.

What I find consistent in each of these cases, is that the members of each family wanted to see their living "Dad" and not what they saw—which was their dad's "dead body." In death we do not look the same because "we" are not there. Our expression, personality, and spark are gone and we look dead, which is what we should look like. In most cases, our personal experiences are limited. When I found my dad slumped over in his wheelchair I knew exactly what I was looking at, I have seen it many times before. Without supportive preparation and, truthfully even with it, it is still difficult.

I believe that one of the most stunning things to see is the body without the expression of life in it. It is very powerful and will cause a reaction by those who see it. Do we think it is bad for us to have this reaction? It is one of the most "normal" reactions there is. We feel sad because we loved someone and now they are gone. That love is a wonderful gift. In fact, the more we loved, the more difficult it may be. Our relationship is directly proportionate to our feelings of loss.

I remember one of my staff being upset about a particular family that was having a difficult time and crying a lot. I asked her what she saw when she looked at this family and she responded, "sadness." I suggested she consider seeing something else, and that was why they were sad: love. They were experiencing sadness because they loved. How wonderful is that, and how lucky for them!

> *They were experiencing sadness because they loved. How wonderful is that, and how lucky for them!*

It is important to realize that in our minds we all want to walk into that room and see the person we know and love, and their presence is not there anymore (new reality). The reaction we experience is the human brain saying, "I don't want this." Most of our reactions are quite normal, but they feel strange or bad because of our inexperience. We have little reference and experience of this new reality and it's not what we're accustomed to feeling.

Often while making arrangements, when the discussion gets to talking about the presence for the body for services, I will get the universal response, "We want to remember him or her as she was."

This is typically an excuse to avoid the potential struggle associated with seeing the dead body. Again, it is not about remembering. It is about acknowledging the death so that our brains can get to work on the important things: where do we go from here: Connection, Reflection and Celebrating.

The funeral director and author, Tom Lynch says in his book The Undertaking, "A good funeral gets the dead where they need to go and the living where they need to be." It brings together family and the stories of our life and its meaning. Yes, we cry, but there can be good feelings attached to those tears. I see it every day. Fear not my friends, trust and be willing to feel. You will not be disappointed.

Chapter Thirteen

Connection

"For the 99 percent of the time we've been on Earth, we were hunter and gatherers, our lives dependent on knowing the fine, small details of our world. Deep inside, we still have a longing to be reconnected with the nature that shaped our imagination, our language, our song and dance, our sense of the divine."
—Janine M. Benyus

Connection—when we are able to be most vulnerable and transparent. The experience of the death of a family member is one of the few guarantees we will have in life. It will happen, I guarantee it, yet it remains an event we continue to struggle with.

Let's take a quick look at the average life experience.

With the United States average life expectancy currently hovering at around 78.88 years, the age to which most Americans can expect to live is still forty-four years younger than the human life span. So how do we close that gap and elongate our lives? There will always be factors that are out of our individual control like our inherited genes, but we shouldn't discount the impact of those that we can control. It is generally understood that closing the gap between life expectancy and life span can be done through healthier living, less exposure to toxins, the prevention of chronic illnesses, and a little bit of luck. The most common cause of death is heart disease.

We all know the common physical symptoms and issues of heart disease, but what is it that causes these physical changes? Science is finally looking at the cause of this breakdown. What is being discovered is that long term fear, frustration, anxiety, and disappointment are significant contributing factors in heart disease. These functions relate to our emotional experience (called hurt), which when activated is asking for the body and mind connection to be healed. If we don't attend to these messages, or if we shut them down so as not to be recognized, our engines (our heart) will break down. In our current state of development, medicine is showing us that the human heart can last about seventy to one hundred years under these conditions.

I believe that Jesus, and others, said thousands of years ago that we all have the ability to live multi-centuries and that our bodies are designed to live this long. It is easy for me to understand the average death rates in the US because the first hundred years are the toughest. In our lifetimes we will lose everyone we have grown to love or care for. We will lose everything; people, pets, animals, jobs, relationships, homes, etc. With the level of technology so advanced, we will lose the world we have grown accustomed to and even mastered, many times.

Our struggle is with our inability to reconcile ourselves with the hurt associated with the loss of our world, and we don't even know it. We are in a constant state of "re-construction" constantly recreating our place in the world of change and loss. When it comes to the loss of a loved one, the funeral has been, and continues to be one of the only effective experiences in our journey towards health and wellbeing since the beginning of time.

Recently, I met with a family member whose father had just died at the age of eighty-six. We had a long conversation about what this event meant, and how it had impacted her and the family as a whole. After some discussion, it was revealed that it had been her father's wish to be immediately cremated. The cremated remains were to be returned to them, and they would have a service in their home town during the summer.

> *Our struggle is with our inability to reconcile ourselves with the hurt associated with the loss of our world, and we don't even know it.*

At that point, summer was still five months away, but waiting was fine with them. It was mentioned during our conversation that just three months earlier, her sister and brother-in-law, along with one of their three children, had died tragically in an automobile accident. Their experience with death in the last few months had been overwhelming in so many ways. At that time, their major concern expressed to me was getting things back to normal for their teenaged nephew and niece, the two remaining living children. Having been given the responsibility of guardianship, they were more concerned for their sister's children than for their need to address the loss of their dad.

Now, I'm not here to pass judgment on them, or anyone else for feeling this way, we all do the best we can do and it is not uncommon to feel many things after the death of an elderly parent. I am here to provide a view as to how we might look at the course of life and death, and in the process, how to best deal with grief and loss.

The first statement I would like to share here is that we cannot return to normal. The way our life was before a loss, whether the loss was tragic or welcomed, will never be the same. It is not possible to return to the life we knew before the loss. In our culture, you will see this appear everywhere we look, and it isn't only about death. One example is job loss. We are living in a time where we all know more people that have lost jobs than ever before. Our culture, and the way it operates, is changing so drastically and quickly that it can leave us spinning aimlessly in shock. I have witnessed many of my friends, as well as others that pursue the same type of job so as to return to their place of "normal," rather than consider attaining new skills and creating new opportunities and a "new normal."

Our world is changing so fast, and the concept of what is normal is changing daily.

Another example is that of the good and hardworking people who have worked in the coal mines. You can see entire towns living in despair, waiting for the mines to once again open so they can return to what they consider their normal life. They wait to return to a life that for now has changed.

Our world is changing so fast, and the concept of what is normal is changing daily. The concept of change and a "new normal" is our reality. Having the emotional fortitude to change with it, although very hard and scary, is paramount in our growth and health.

Let's return to the story about the family with the teenagers whose parents and sister had died in a tragic accident. This family's life had been torn apart. The mirror that reflected back their image of reality was missing three and now four people in it in the matter of months. How would they deal with their reconstruction, creating the new normal, the new family image in their mirrors?

We all are left with the task of reconstructing our lives, reconstructing and creating our new normal. It can be an arduous task but one we cannot escape.

Although I am using this specific story here, there are many, many more families who will and continue to do the same thing. My suggestion to them and to you is to go through every challenge we're given no matter how hard It may appear and do it at the earliest convenience. We have a resolve a place within all of us that once exposed, shines the light on just how powerful and beautiful life is and can be. And we have a place in it; it is here for us to experience.

My suggestion was, "Wouldn't it be a better solution to bring those two surviving children to town to gather in the loving arms of their cousins, aunts, and uncles while acknowledging the death of their grandfather? Wouldn't it be a good idea for the older surviving children to experience the loss of their dad together with their children and close friends and community now"?

We don't put off birthdays, anniversaries, holidays, weddings, or births, yet we feel compelled to put off the one thing we can guarantee in life. If we continue to deny the opportunity to return to a healthy functioning state—after a stressful situation when it's needed most—we place ourselves and our health in jeopardy.

> *We don't put off birthdays, anniversaries, holidays, weddings, or births, yet we feel compelled to put off the one thing we can guarantee in life.*

Is there a way that we can rise above that, allowing us to live each day and thrive in the new normal, or present, condition? Often when we have struggles in life we rely on our fight and flight survival mechanism by relying on the human brain to figure a way out. I am here to tell you that, yes, it is a good tool, and when our life is threatened, we are glad it's there. However, it is not our friend when we are experiencing loss, at a time when we need to have the mind and heart working together in a natural harmony.

I believe the solution is a heart-based experience, bringing together our community of family and friends at a time when it's needed. In doing this, it connects us with the meaning of life: "the funeral." For it is the funeral occasion that teaches us the power of mourning, the practice of expressing your grief outside of yourself. Allowing for people to care, allowing for the reality to reconstruct and allowing for us to express our grief without judgment because it is sad and appropriate to feel sad then. We will mourn for the rest of our lives.

We often feel overwhelmed in life, where we're "going through the motions" and doing as well as is possible. We all have had those moments, and I don't want to give you the impression that there's anything wrong with that. It happens. If we can see this overwhelming experience as a sign of something that needs our attention, then we might find a way to move through those feeling towards a healthier outcome. If we can't, we might experience symptoms such as depression, problems sleeping, and physical pain. Some may also experience a compulsion towards eating, drinking and drugs. Other symptoms include crying uncontrollably and responses of anger and negativity.

In a recent Gannett newspaper article, according to government data, it's been reported that one thousand Iraq and Afghanistan era veterans are being diagnosed with Post Traumatic Stress Disorder every week. That's right, every week. The study's review released last year concluded that the Pentagon and Department of Veterans Affairs were struggling to keep pace with a growing number of mental health problems generated by the wars. They have spent millions of dollars on developing coping strategies, fitness programs, and help in cultivating strong social relationships.

It has cost $125 million to teach these coping skills to one million soldiers. A scientific panel selected to review the program has said there is little or no evidence that the program prevents mental illness. Not to sound foolish here, but attempting to train people to be resilient to killing people in war through government programs by developing coping strategies seems counter intuitive to me. It sounds to me like what we need here is a good funeral, something to help our soldiers grieve and mourn the loss of many things.

The rise in statistics for stress-related conditions in the military and in the United States as a whole is not a surprise when we take into account the daily stresses we encounter in life. Yet in the presence of life affirming emotions such as compassion, gratitude, caring, and appreciation, the brain releases life-affirming hormones that produce significant benefits.

> *In each moment of our day, there is a constant conversation between the heart and the brain.*

In each moment of our day, there is a constant conversation between the heart and the brain. The reason this connection is so important is that the quality of these emotions affect the hormones released and directly relate to the quality of our lives. Meaning, the quality of our "emotions" determines the instructions our hearts send to our brains, which in turn affects our behavior. It is when we are in this space of balance and connection between the heart and brain that we create a place of peace, compassion, and gratitude.

It is a place where all things are possible. It is that place where unconditional love lives, that which I have been searching for my whole life.

Chapter Fourteen

Alone

"All through the long winter, I dream of my garden.
On the first day of spring, I dig my fingers deep into
the soft earth. I can feel its energy, and my spirits soar."
—*Helen Hayes*

Probably one of the most profound things I've learned about dying is that we all die alone. I didn't want to accept this because of how sad and scary this seems to be. I would like my loved ones to be surrounded by family, because one of my greatest fears is to be alone. Throughout life, our human hearts want to be connected, loved, cared for etc. So the thought of someone we love doing this alone is heart-wrenching.

The truth is; we are the only ones on that journey

and no one can do it for us, or with us. You may have the privilege to be there as I was with my mother and father, but you may not. The timing, and whether or not we get to be present, is beyond our control. Although for many this is a very depressing and unwelcome idea, when understood it can be very comforting. Do not let your hearts be troubled, as they may not be alone at all (which I'll speak to shortly).

I had the personal experience with my own grandmother's death. As a young child, I lived with both her and my dad from the age of three until I was six. I remember vividly the many nights at our lake house where she would sit with me for what seemed like hours massaging my legs that kept me awake at night.

After graduating from mortuary school, I lived in one of the bedrooms in her house behind the funeral home. I was a companion for her as much as she was to me. Daily I looked forward to lunch with her while watching her favorite soap operas.

She was like a mother to me. I loved her very much.

At the age of ninety-three, she struggled for ten days in her effort of leaving this world. I found it difficult to watch her struggle, and I thought I might be able to help. I had heard how some people had helped family members exit peacefully from the world we know and into the next. I thought that because of my experience and love for her that I, too, could help.

One afternoon, I got in bed with her eighty-seven-pound body and held her tenderly in my arms. I whispered very quietly in her ear that I was with her and that I loved her. And then, in a moment of quiet contemplation and hope, I whispered softly in her ear that it was ok for her to go.

The next few moments were ones that I will never forget. Somehow, this unresponsive, eighty-seven-pound, ninety-three-year-old grandmother, who I loved very much and who loved me, turned almost violently towards me and with one giant checking elbow move was able to propel me to the floor from her bed. Now, I'm not a little guy and it was not easy to toss me from her bed. In that moment it became clear to me that she was not ready to go. In fact, she apparently had more work to do before it was her time.

She died quietly five days later at 2:00 in the morning. I was called to her bedside that night and I could tell that she was no longer there. Although we were sad, I felt good that she had worked it out, whatever it was, and it felt good that she was no longer suffering or in pain. To be honest, I believe that the final days before our death can be a house cleaning of sorts, as I would not be surprised if my grandmother needed to make amends for shortcomings in her mind related to relationships or actions. The times she lived in were tough times, and we're not all perfect.

There are struggles that we all go through in life, and in our death we have the opportunity to work them out if necessary. This is the experience that I call Hell, the place we go to, in and during dying. My recommendation is that we do the work, or reconcile, before we die. Good luck with that!!

I know that my grandmother's life was a hard one. But I never heard her complain (unless it was regarding the price of bread or something). She was the glue that held our family together. She was one of the hardest workers I have known. Although she may have not have been famous or financially successful, she taught us all the values of hard work, the value of putting family first and putting a hot meal on the table on time. Through her example, she provided the data, the road map we needed to live a good life.

She had lived a long and productive life and we would acknowledge that.

My aunt had lived most of her life in Florida where she had a family of five daughters to care for. But in the months leading up to my grandmother's death, she had been my grandmother's primary caregiver. I remember a time when she decided to take her into the hospital one night. Nancy and I were getting ready for bed when the call came. After explaining her condition, I agreed that it sounded like a good idea and asked her to keep us posted. As soon as I hung up the phone, my wife asked me why I wasn't going to the hospital. After a moment of thought, I shared with Nancy that my aunt was going to be there and she would keep us posted, and this seemed reasonable to me. Nancy pointed out that my aunt shouldn't be alone if something were to happen, and that I should go. I was tired, and I wanted to go to bed! But on this night, I learned an important lesson about life. If there is ever any question as to whether you think you should go or not, GO!!!

You cannot imagine the power of presence; the truth is you can always come home.

On this night it was determined that my grandmother had a bowel obstruction and that surgery was recommended. My aunt and I were asked to make the decision about the surgery and we decided against it. Had I not been there, she would have had to live with her decision of determining her mother's fate alone. Instead, I was there with her sharing that moment and I knew we were making the right decision. My grandmother died the next month.

Although it was her two living sons, Ben and George, who started the funeral home, it was her daughter Margaret (my aunt) and I who planned and coordinated the services. One of Margaret's personal requests was that we have Alice Blue Gown, a favorite and meaningful song, played at the funeral. Alice

Blue Gown was a song from the Broadway show Irene, and the story goes that my grandfather took my grandmother to the show and hired a car (which was a big deal in those days). My grandmother and her brother Henry, who had also been in attendance at the show, had sung that song many times during her life and it played an important part in my Aunt Margaret's memory.

Unfortunately, the minister would not allow it in the liturgy of the funeral service. The minister tried to explain something about it being a Broadway tune, and not appropriate in the church's funeral rites and protocols. After a rather heated and lengthy conversation, we managed to agree to bringing her casket into the church in a procession while a local tenor sang the song. The church service officially began after the procession so as not to offend their "protocols." Needless to say, these little distractions can add significant drama to a family in grief. But it's these moments that I think I enjoy the most because of the challenges they bring. There's always a way if you're willing to do the work and not bow down to indifference.

Living and Dying

Chapter Fifteen

Reflection

"The purpose of life is undoubtedly to know oneself.
We cannot do it unless we learn to identify ourselves
with all that lives. The sum-total of that life is God."
—*Mahatma Gandhi*

Reflection—deeply considering the things that matter most in life.

One cannot discuss living and dying without reflecting and connecting with the concept of a Supreme Being, a Universal Consciousness, God, and the concept of Heaven. Over the course of my career, I have made it a practice to research and study religious as well as non-religious concepts and ideas. I have read the Bible cover to cover, studied with Bible groups, and private spiritual groups. I have read many different philosophers and spiritual authors' thoughts on the concept of God and spirit. To my delight, in many instances, what I was reading and hearing was like listening to my own thoughts. When I heard something that resonated with something that I intuitively knew or felt inside me, it was inspiring.

Having not experienced strong connections with my birth mother, stepmother, or my father, I was primed for discovering new and supportive concepts of unconditional love. It was suggested in most of my material that God was the epitome of unconditional love, which to me was highly motivating. I couldn't help but think, "Wouldn't it be cool to know him?" I was once like a lot of people in the world wanting to be shown proof of God. I wanted proof that there was such a thing as a soul. I struggled with love and with the concept of God as a Supreme Being.

Since I never really had an experience with unconditional love on a parental level, as my birth mother had left me, my step mother was never a factor and my father never seemed satisfied with me, I felt alone and on my own. One of my greatest gifts in my journey of finding unconditional love was the marriage to my wife and the birth of our children. She taught me how to say, "I love you" out loud, and she helped me in my growth as a loving and caring spouse and father.

My relationship with my birth mother was rekindled when my dad arranged a time for my wife and me to meet with her in the early nineteen eighties. At the time, Nancy was pregnant with our first child. It was an amazing time in my life to have this fantasy play out right before my eyes.

Unfortunately, I truly believe that every time my mother saw me for the next twenty years prior to her death that it brought back memories of her personal experience with the Anthony family. This would often put a strain on our relationship in the years to come on both sides. To my great delight, I can honestly say that in the six months prior to her death that she had somehow made amends with her issues with her past. For the first time in my life I could sense and really feel the unconditional love of my mother. I feel blessed to have experienced that. Since her death, I have come to intuitively know that a mothers always there even if it was not in our everyday awareness.

The truth that I have learned is that the heart connection is always calling, laying there, waiting for us to hear it. It does not sit in condemnation, judgments or any of the other many mental activities we engage in daily. It exists only in love, and we were lovingly given the keys to that kingdom months before she died.

But this does not always happen. Many families come to me with broken hearts and relationships every day. I have witnessed fist fights, temper tantrums, and damaging words exchanged in the heat of this emotional time. I have witnessed the healing effects of forgiveness. I also have witnessed the overwhelmingly loving and caring families that we all wish to be a part of. I know their lives have not always been picture perfect, but they have found a way to accept each other's differences. I have come to learn that there is always a strong leader in that family (often a parent) who is a living presence and model of unconditional love, a strong heart centered individual that leads the way.

When I get the opportunity to conduct graveside services, I reference the idea that we bury what we can't have and don't need anymore, and we take away from this place all that is good, to carry with us until we meet again.

Often in arrangements, I hear stories of how the person who died had been so "demented" or "out of it" that they thought they were talking to their parents or other deceased relatives. While I'm not a medium who can talk to the dearly departed, I do believe they may indeed be talking to them. Over my lifetime, I have had experiences that make me believe there is another realm that we journey to—another realm of energy vibration, more accessible to those in between worlds.

Three books I have read recently speak to this through the author's personal experiences: *Proof of Heaven*, written by a neurosurgeon, Eben Alexander M.D., *Dying to be Me*, written by Anita Moojani, and *Heaven is for Real*, an interview with Colton Burpo's dad, Todd Burpo. All three of these books address the personal experiences each writer had with dying and being transported to a new and wonderful place.

After some extensive reading, research, and personal encounters, I have determined that when we die, there is a transition that takes place from this world to the next. Sometimes the transition takes place slowly, and sometimes the transition is fast. In the event of a slower transition, it is not uncommon to have deceased loved ones, family, friends, etc., visit us to help make our transition more comfortable and less fearful.

I have witnessed loved ones carrying on conversations with deceased relatives while I was in the room. They became frustrated with me because I was unable to see them as they did. I listen to countless families repeat similar stories and share their unique experiences with dates, music, and strange occurrences that occur to them, all of which provides more evidence to me that there is something beyond this physical existence.

One of the most profound experiences happened to me within the last year. I was called at home in the early morning by a friend whose mother had just died. We had talked many times over the preceding weeks as her condition worsened. She was finding it difficult to let go. It's as if there was some internal struggle keeping her here. As I was driving to the nursing home, I had this remarkable clairvoyant experience. I pictured a small room with two large doors at one end of the room and a long bench on the right wall as I looked at the doors. There was a young man sitting on the bench, bent over, with his face in his hands as if he was struggling with, or worried about, something. He was wearing khaki pants, a short sleeve white shirt unbuttoned at the top and white socks. My friend's mom appeared in this room as a young girl in her late teens or early twenties. She was wearing a tight sweater top and a 50s style poodle skirt (I didn't see any poodle on it though).

As she walked into the room, the young man rose to his feet and reached out his hand to her with a sense of relief and big smile and escorted her through the closed double doors. Inside the doors was a large room, gymnasium style, with fifty to seventy-five people gathered at the far wall clapping and cheering as she and her young man danced their way into the hall. I had to pull over as the most intense feeling of peace and joy had me crying like a baby. I believe I had just been witness to how she transitioned over and I had, more importantly, been given the opportunity to experience the feeling that came with it. As I told the story to her son only moments later, I once again was moved to tears as I shared my experience with him. It was good. This experience, once again, confirmed my belief of a new and wonderful place we all will someday come to know.

Science has proven there's a field of energy that underlies all physical existence. This field is so new in its discovery that scientists have yet to agree upon a single term. It's been called everything from "the field," to "the mind of God," to "nature's mind." In 1944, Max Planck, the father of quantum theory, called it "the matrix," and more recently the "God particle."

For a moment in time I had the experience of connecting with this field. I highly recommend it.

Chapter Sixteen

Consciousness

"If there is one thing clear about the centuries dominated by the factory and the wheel, it is that although the machine can make everything from a spoon to a landing-craft, a natural joy in earthly living is something it never has and never will be able to manufacture."
—Henry Beston

Consciousness of this energy as a reality in the universe is, I believe, one of the hardest ideas to grasp. Because it is invisible to most of our regularly used senses, it can seem abstract to our mind. Yet you can feel or sense it, and I believe it is both the cause and creator of all things in our life. For years, I wondered why people didn't "get it," why everyone couldn't see auras, or why people struggled with the concepts of infinity and the idea of consciousness. What I've learned is that we each see the world through our own lens; it's like watching a movie of our creation based on our interpretations, past experiences, and thoughts. In addition to the movie, there exists a radio station that is playing the songs of our soul, the songs of our creation. It is only that we do not have our radio tuned into that station that we do not hear the music.

A book titled "Biocentrism: How Life and Consciousness Are the Keys to Understanding the Nature of the Universe" has stirred up the Internet because it contains a notion that life does not end when the body dies and that it can last forever. The author of this publication, scientist Dr. Robert Lanza, who was voted the third most important scientist alive by the NY Times, has no doubts that this is possible.[3]

Ralph Waldo Emerson wrote:

---

3 See more at: http://www.spiritscienceandmetaphysics.com/scientists-claim-that-quantum-theory-proves-consciousness-moves-to-another-universe-at-death/#sthash.J6uoeTBq.dpuf

We have learned that we do not see directly, but mediately, and that we have no means of correcting these colored and distorting lenses which we are, or of computing the amount of their errors. Perhaps these subject-lenses have a creative power; perhaps there are no objects. Once we lived in what we saw, now, the rapaciousness of this new power, which threatens to absorb all things, engages us. Nature, art, persons, letters, religions, — objects, successively tumble in, and God is but one of its ideas. Nature and litera-ture are subjective phenomena; every evil and every good thing is a shadow which we cast. The street is full of humiliations to the proud. As the fop contrived to dress his bailiffs in his livery, and make them wait on his guests at table, so the chagrins which the bad heart gives off as bubbles, at once take form as ladies and gentlemen in the street, shop men or barkeepers in hotels, and threaten or insult whatever is threatenable and insultable in us. 'Tis the same with our idolatries. People forget that it is the eye which makes the horizon, and the rounding mind's eye which makes this or that man a type or representative of humanity with the name of hero or saint. Jesus the "providential man," is a good man on whom many people are agreed that these optical laws shall take effect.[4]

I believe that our souls live eternally and continue to live even after we pass from this world. What makes our soul live eternally? Energy. Our soul is energy, and that energy is the part of us that lives forever. The physical body we are given in each lifetime is simply the creation of our mind, a form for our energy body, our soul to express itself. When a soul becomes a human body, it gives that body life. When the soul leaves that human body, it no longer has life. Every living thing is created, sustained and given life by the energy of a soul.

We are energy. It is energy that sustains and maintains our entire existence. Many people believe that

---

4 http://www.emersoncentral.com/experience.htm

life is supported by our heart, lungs and other organs alone. While our organs and physical body do keep us up and running, it is our energy body that gives life to them. Our energy body sustains our physical body. Energy is the common medium of your mind, emotions, body, and soul. To me, and I hope to you, the examination of new ideas and experiences can be the springboard to a new fulfillment, joy and peace in our lives. Although for many it may be too difficult a journey to imagine, do not give up. I believe there is a new dawn, a new beginning for all of us and that time is rapidly approaching.

In my opinion, and in the opinion of Greg Braden, New York Times best-selling author and scientist; an obsolete paradigm of the universe and our relationship to it was based upon a series of scientific assumptions—false assumptions—that can no longer be taught as fact in light of new evidence. Examples of these include the following:

- **False Assumption 1:** Civilization is approximately 5,000 to 5,500 years old.

- **False Assumption 2:** Nature is based upon "survival of the fittest."

- **False Assumption 3:** Random events of evolution explain human origins.

- **False Assumption 4:** Consciousness is separate from our physical world.

- **False Assumption 5:** The space between things is empty.

While I cannot provide the evidence and speak to all of these assumptions today, I will focus on the nature based ideas that are closest to my heart and correspond to my work professionally.

In the late 1800s, Charles Darwin brought something new to the old philosophy, a plausible idea called "natural selection." Natural selection, with its emphasis on death and competition, did not appeal to some naturalists because they felt it was immoral and left little room for the concept of progress in the development of life. This new idea, however, gave birth to the concept of "survival of the fittest," which was widely accepted in our world and to a large degree continues to this day. The problem as I see it is that the survival of the fittest model breeds discontent, competition, aggression and war, contrary to what we find in nature.

According to Gregg Braden, "Darwinian evolution doesn't work." Although "survival of the fittest" has always been accepted as the standard for biological behavior, Braden says that we are more inclined toward peace than war and that we are more wired for cooperative existence and mutual aid than competition. Even more important to how we handle the coming societal changes  is his discussion of nature's propensity toward cooperation and mutual aid instead of "survival of the fittest" biological competition—in other words, he says, Darwin was wrong. The new scientific model is based on cooperation.

He goes on to say that between the years 1998

and 2000, four hundred studies were designed to identify the optimum amount of violent competition in a species. They looked at numerous varieties of species and the findings were consistent—the optimal amount of competition is "zero." They found that cooperation among species is what insures their survival. The only way we can successfully make this transition is to examine and rid ourselves of our notions of "Darwinian competition," and we must learn to cooperate and help each other. This needs to happen at every level and on a global scale. This isn't only about how do I cooperate with my mother-in-law, my next door neighbors, and with others I deal with in business. It is also about how nations cooperate with other nations.

The best example of the natural state of cooperation in nature is the human body. The human body has over fifty trillion cells operating in a constant state of cooperation every second. If we were to have a state of aggression and competition in the body, we would generate disease and break down. As you will see, our bodies are dramatically affected by our thoughts, beliefs, and actions.

When we think about everyday life—the way we care for ourselves and our families, how we solve our problems, the choices we make—we find that much of what we accept as common knowledge is rooted in the core beliefs of these false assumptions. Many of our core beliefs are holdovers of an outdated science that began three hundred years ago. It may be no coincidence that during this same period of time, the world has found itself facing the greatest crises of war, suffering, and disease in recorded history. These ideas of our sterile-sounding chemical origins, of our relatively recent arrival on Earth, and of our separateness from nature, have led us to believe that we're little more than specks of dust in the universe and a biological sidebar in the overall scheme of life.

Is it any wonder that we often feel powerless to help our loved ones and ourselves when we face life's great crises? Is it any wonder that we often feel just as helpless when we see our world changing so fast that it has been described as "falling apart at the seams?" At first blush, there seems to be no reason for us to think any differently, no reason for us to believe that we have any control over ourselves or the events in our lives. After all, there's nothing in our traditional textbooks or old-fashioned way of seeing the world that allows for anything else.

Chapter Seventeen

Celebration

"I am in love with this world . . . I have climbed its mountains, roamed its forests, sailed its waters, crossed its deserts, felt the sting of its frosts, the oppression of its heats, the drench of its rains, the fury of its winds, and always have beauty and joy waited upon my goings and comings."
—John Burroughs

Celebrating—making room for joy. Who doesn't want to celebrate or have joy in their life?

I have recently participated in Neale Donald Walsh's course, "Living from your soul." Neale is the author of the book Conversations with God. In one of the sessions, he speaks to my concept of living in joy. His interpretation of living in joy is to live in a state of "creation." To me, creation means living in a place of gratitude and acknowledging that all things are possible (hopefully that idea brings a smile to your face). He also goes on to show how by moving a few letters around, the word creation can easily be manipulated to read as "reaction" (The other option). I would go so far as to say that we have the choice of living in one or the other, but most often we don't realize it is a choice.

> *To me, creation means living in a place of gratitude and acknowledging that all things are possible*

In the everyday life of funeral service I see this challenge regularly. I see families embrace their love for each other and pass through "the shadow of the valley of death" easily. I see others react and fight it out.

In the funeral experience today, we are witnessing a movement towards re-wording our public notices to include "a celebration of life" The funeral has always been a celebration of life with all the trappings.

Personally, I do not have a problem with any of

this as long as we don't skip the work of grieving and mourning the loss. Based on my observation, it is not humanly possible to celebrate a life when you have not come to terms with its ending, its meaning and its effect on you. The very real celebration comes only after we've have processed all of the unfinished business that relationships breed. The true celebration of life comes after we have cried, reached out, gathered, hugged, eaten lots of food, shared memories, cried, yelled, forgiven, and processed all of the events that had been left unresolved.

> *The true celebration of life comes after we have cried, reached out, gathered, hugged, eaten lots of food, shared memories, cried, yelled, forgiven, and processed all of the events that had been left unresolved.*

The easier option is to avoid anything that will make us feel bad. I cannot begin to tell you how many families struggle with the idea of feeling anything. As I have said before, if we do not exhaust the myriad of emotions and thoughts about loss from our bodies, it will break down. Our bodies were made to purge from us those things we should not suppress! We were designed to handle it.

The death of a loved one is an open door for healing, growth and personal development. It is one of the most significant life events we will ever experience. I believe that true celebrating takes place after we purge ourselves of any and all trash we need to put out. In my dad's case, the last thirteen years of his life living with his disability was very hard on me, the eldest son. When he died, I had to do the work of purging the pain and suffering (the reaction) related to that. Once I did that, I was on the road to recovery. It took me a couple of days, but after that work I was able to recall all of the really good years of growing up and bring that to the celebration of his life, unclouded by the recent painful past (creation). I make it a point not to say this a lot as it can be misunderstood, but my dad's funeral was one of the highlights of my life.

I've always had a problem with funeral services where it felt like someone was just reading words from a book. In my familiarity I knew that at my dad's service, every word spoken would have a specific meaning and resonate with me because I was involved in every detail. When it came to readings from the Bible, I used a Bible with a concordance. The concordance provides a description of qualities such as forgiveness (which I specifically needed) and where the concept would appear in the Bible. I picked a reading from the New and Old Testament and was able to encourage family friends to assist in reading them. My dad was an active Rotarian all of his life and I picked the song "America" to be sung during the service.

For those of you who know Rotarians, they love to sing. I remember one point during the song when I stopped singing and just stood and listened. There were at least fifty Rotarians in the church, and they were in rare form. The service lasted an hour and fifteen minutes which is unheard of in the Presbyterian Church, but because of all the elements, participation, and three of us presenting eulogies, it lasted a long time (it felt like twenty minutes). I am often taken back when I hear clergy suggest limiting the participation of the family and friends partly due to time constraints. The reality here is this, there is no amount of time where one can adequately capture a life, and instead we're asked to capture life's essence, a difficult thing to do in a short amount of time.

I have been to services where the family member has gone on with a eulogy for forty-five minutes, a painful experience. I felt bad for the family as the son must have repeated himself and told the same story many times (in this case I was willing to handle the hook personally). I was at another service of a very well know family and a full church where after the son's eulogy the deceased's brother felt moved to say a few words. The priest came down off the altar, physically turned the brother around and told him to sit down. This all happened in front of four hundred people and in this case, I was ready to run to the defense of the brother.

There are many other stories of families wanting to be engaged and being upset by clergy and church doctrine, leaving them with little options and wanting more. I have learned to intervene and make suggestions in this struggle because it is our desire to honor this time with words of love and respect. Unfortunately, establishing precedents in our church affects what we have to do for others.

My solution is to encourage families to use multiple venues for participation. There can be many opportunities created for honoring our connections in life either at the funeral home, church, cemetery or reception. If there is only one event, it can limit our opportunity.

Military funerals are a remarkable experience and a sight to see. If any organization truly understands the privilege of attending to a ceremony celebrating life, it's the military. I don't care what branch or what age, the military does it right. There is an understanding of life and death on a very fundamental and real level in the military. They understand the sanctity of life,

> *There is an understanding of life and death on a very fundamental and real level in the military.*

they understand the meaning of ceremony, and they understand reverence to death. If you have ever had the opportunity to witness a full military funeral, you know what I mean.

We've had the unfortunate task of attending to

many military funerals at our firm. The most recent experience was memorable in that the local airport manager and security team had me over in advance to review the procedures in receiving the remains from overseas. We arrived at the designated time with our hearse and staff, and were escorted onto the airfield. When the plane arrived, the family was on the tarmac with our staff, the airport dignitaries, security team, airport fire department, and the local sheriff's department.

As the plane came to a stop at the gate and shut down its engine, the military escort was asked to deplane and the passengers asked to wait to deplane until after the deceased veteran was transferred from the cargo hold. As I sit here today I can remember the tears welling in my eyes as I experienced the gratitude of a nation receiving a fallen soldier home. There was not a dry eye in the airport who witnessed this, and I can assure you it will not be forgotten by anyone there

The services for this Army officer took place over three days. A platoon of officers and enlisted men in attendance had specific instructions for attending to the family, our staff and the deceased veteran who had died in battle. I was so impressed with their attention to detail and their willingness to serve this honor of burial, that I spent extra time training and practicing with them on the specific details so I didn't feel the need to have my trained staff involved. It was with gratitude, honor, and duty that these fine men and women performed their roles. If we could learn anything from the military, it's the way they deal with their dead: with respect, gratitude, honor, and duty.

Chapter Eighteen

Preplanning

"It was in the forest that I found the peace that passes all understanding."
—Jane Goodall

M any people these days are running to funeral homes for the act of pre-planning their own funerals. One of the main motivators is the peace of mind that comes from putting aside money to pay for their own funerals before their resources run out. In the event that an individual needs full time nursing care, it is possible to exhaust all of their funds in this extensive care situation over time. Because of that, the government in most states allows them to put aside burial funds to cover their own funeral expenses.

Another reason why families want to pre-plan their funerals is quite simply the peace of mind. While preplanning is a significant and positive effort to help families, it can also be a way of sabotaging the survivor's needs and desires when the actual death event is experienced.

Funerals are for the living. We are the ones left behind. We are the ones affected by the loss and we are the ones with the needs. We are the ones that should be involved with the decisions.

Funerals are for the living. We are the ones left behind.

Why is it that the dying should get to make all the decisions? Although I have not heard this sentiment often in my daily work, I do feel that it is of major significance. I believe that for many, this discussion is an uncomfortable one, or at least they think it will be, so it's avoided at all costs. Who really wants to talk about our mom or dad dying? Yet this is the one thing we can guarantee. You've heard the saying, "We don't get out of life alive."

Many years ago, I had to moderate a discussion

between my wife and mother-in-law. My mother-in-law, who is a wonderfully delightful woman, is currently working as a social worker at the age of eighty-five. It is her desire that her body be donated to the university medical center. As I remember it, there was a discussion between mother and daughter expressing these views.

The thoughts were shared in the context of, "This is my wish and you will follow my wishes. In fact, I demand you do this as it is my right to have done with me what I want!" This situation throws a light on the responsibility of a child to honor their parent's wishes, although the legal rights actually lie with the children, family, or designated guardian to do as they wish. While I can understand her desire for body donation, being associated to the university created a conflict between the two women.

My wife Nancy, having been a mortuary student, has seen the medical centers facility for cadavers and does not share her mother's fondness for the idea. After all, this is her mother who she has known all her life, who raised and cared for her, and if she is bothered by this thought, why should she be made to feel pressured into doing something upsetting. Why should she be made to feel her needs are not important? Why should she be made to do something that could haunt her for the rest of her years?

In the world I am familiar with, the family dynamics always play a part in decision making and planning for funerals. If we have a close, caring and respectful family unit, there is an inherent feeling of honor and respect towards everyone's thoughts and concerns. You will find family members thoughtfully listening to all the information I share with them, and then they work together to find the perfect solution that meets everyone's needs and comfort levels. If we have a fractured or dysfunctional family, you will find bickering and fighting, family members not speaking to each other (may have been this way for years), and everyone looking for the easiest way out of this situation so as not to have to interact.

Now, I have put out the two extremes here knowing that all of you will react to this. In fact, I feel that it's safe to say that we all may have at least some of the above elements in our own family, but it seems to be leaning more towards dysfunction these days. My next book will be about how to navigate this, but for now suffice it to say that we can only do our best.

A good friend of mine, after an evening of libation and good times, took me aside to confide in me his personal story about his dad's death (I often get pulled aside like this). His dad died unexpectedly and the day before his death, he had called his son in hopes of getting together. We've all heard this same story about not being available but in this instance it was because of work. His dad died the next day and for three years he had been carrying the thought of,"I wish I had found the time to be with him". This thought had slowly grown into a massive burden that he carried. I believe this is a common story as our lives can change in the blink of an eye, and it is a challenge of living that we all carry. Harry Chapin said it best in his song, "Cats in the Cradle."

In the song he speaks of the journey with his dad from childhood to adulthood. This journey takes him from a place of connection with his dad in his childhood to disconnection as an adult. His adult life becomes too busy to spend time with his aging father and closes with a sad ending.

Perhaps we all have a story that in some way mirrors that song, but when we are given the opportunity to recognize it; we need to do something about it. In the story about my friend, I suggested he take some time out of his day when he returned home to go to the cemetery and tell his dad how he felt. Take the time to put it out there so that all can hear. Trust that it will do the work that is needed. Find a way to meet your individual needs, even if the family is against it. You can do it privately and in countless different ways. If you can think it and are able to verbalize it, I will almost guarantee that any good funeral professional can assist you in accomplishing just about anything. If you have a story your carrying around with you, get out there and do the work, you will thank me for it. Oh yes, and good luck!

Preplanning opens a dialogue designed to be helpful, but in some cases it can be very hurtful. We never know how death comes to us and we never can anticipate all of the needs we may have at the time. Without knowledge, some goodwill, and flexibility, you can end up with a real mess. Most often, I find that there is a good compromise for every situation that typically involves doing multiple things. Remember, there is not always an easy "one size fits all" answer.

The most positive scenario is to have a frank and honest discussion about funeral and burial wishes as a family, but only after gathering data and information from a respected funeral professional. The point of allowing the funeral professionals to share different perspectives with you will be life changing.

In my case, in over nearly forty years of service, I have served thousands of individuals and families as they navigate this event. There is no one more qualified to provide you with information on the merits and meanings of the different rituals involving death. Being that the average person's involvement is so limited regarding the purpose of funerals and funeral arranging, it would be foolish to make decisions without the proper knowledge and expertise of your funeral director. Ultimately, it is your family's decision as to what happens, and I can assure you that if you spend the time required to research and develop a plan, you will be well served.

It has been my general experience in preplanning with individuals that are open to discussion, that they all leave our meeting with a completely different view of the options and the meanings that affect the overall outcome of their funeral experience. It is one of the joys of serving the public to see people open and grow in their understanding. The way it appears to me is that they come to me with a heaviness and burden about them, a fear and trepidation that I have the opportunity to dismiss, I have the means to help them cast off their burden. The ones who embrace the opportunity and open themselves up to be vulnerable are the ones that experience the freedom—I watch them leave on tiptoes as if they're walking on air.

This transformation and connection comes to everyone who walks through our doors and opens themselves up to the care, love, and knowledge we are so eager to share. It happens easier in the preplanning event because there is no significant trauma yet, but it can also happen after the most horrific events, like the loss of a child. I have been witness to this,

I know what I speak of, and it is a fact. We all can hope to experience this transformation for ourselves, and it is my most sincere wish for you.

The discussion you can have with your family does not have to be personal. It can be an informal discussion with children, spouses, etc., where the different options of the funeral experience are discussed. You don't even have to make it a group discussion, as this can sometimes cause it to feel odd. Don't make it about you, let it be a frank discussion regarding things like church and spiritual beliefs, burial of the body or cremation and burial, gathering as a community of family and friends, or whatever else comes up. Talk about what they have seen, what they think about, and what they don't like or what makes sense to them.

I'll guarantee that once the ice is broken, it will be easier than you think. After breaking the ice, and at another place and time, consider discussion about beliefs and hopes.

Another way of looking at it is to have the talk of a lifetime. You have a lot to give and can be an inspiration to your loved ones in this activity. Just do it before someone is sick or on their deathbed, as that throws some more anxious energy into the discussion. This could also be a discussion about your experiences with them, what they have meant to you in your lives, and what your life has meant to you. I call it cleaning out the garage. We have all done this as it needs to be done on occasion, and we always feel better when it's done. Again, don't forget to involve your funeral professional and good luck!

Check list:

1. Remember this event is for your family or significant others not you. You will be Ok (trust me), they might have a struggle.

2. Encourage your loved ones to consider any plans you might offer as a guide or road map. They can change as needed to fit their specific needs at the time. Remember the event of death can be a traumatic event requiring unique and special care.

3. Encourage your family to have the

guest of honor (you) present for
services.

4. Encourage gatherings, storytelling,
   pictures, special music, special
   passages, poems and anything that
   will bring with it good feelings.

5. Encourage a final resting place
   whether burial or cremation. We
   all deserve a place on this earth that
   acknowledges and memorializes our
   life.

6. Encourage participation. It is through
   participation that we receive value.

7. Experience life and experience death.

e=motion

"In the woods, we return to reason and faith.
There I feel that nothing can befall me in life.
- no disgrace, no calamity (leaving me my
eyes), which in nature cannot repair."
—Ralph Waldo Emerson

Now that we have "cleaned out the garage," it's time to do what I lovingly call, "take your temperature." On a regular basis in the journey through grief and the funeral event, I check in with families to see how they're doing. I "take their temperature." It is that time in the process of my connection with you, the reader. As I look around the field of experience and energy in the world, I see movement towards a new and exciting place. It brings with it feelings of trepidation but underlying our fear, I sense a feeling of hope. It is as if our place in the world has moved a little because it may feel a little odd and strange.

It is a gray and rainy day where I sit today. The trees are just beginning to bud, and you can feel and smell that Spring is here. The birds wake me up each morning, and I watch their excitement and exuberance at the feeder. Any day now, life will burst through the binding that holds it and bring with it a new expression of the same life that has always been there, always connected but hidden from our view through the winter months. I remember last year, and the years before, where I had the same feelings and thoughts, yet I hope that somehow today I will grow and blossom into a better place.

As I look around the field of experience and energy in the world, I see movement towards a new and exciting place.

While my view of the world outside reflects the darkness in my mind and darkness in the world around me, I know that if I can find a new thought to hang on to, a new place of hope, a hopeful connection, perhaps I can escape from the damp and dreary hole of self despair. You see, it is the memory of new life that highlights my connection with despair, and I need to remind myself that it is only a thought, a memory of the past. If I can change my thought, I can change my world. When I look out into the world today I can choose to see only new life. I will choose not to accept the memory of despair, because that is not what is real for me today. It is only a trap of my mind, a memory of the past.

> *If I can change my thought, I can change my world.*

When we think of our loved ones that have gone before us, choose to hold that connection with the memory of their love, but choose to frame it in a new way. I had a minister frame it at the funeral of a young friend by using an airport metaphor. He referred to his death by saying, "He just got on an earlier flight." I liked the metaphor because it affirmed that at some point I, too, would be making that same flight, and that I would see him again.

173

The process of holding onto a belief and the hope of new life in nature, both in our outer and inner world, is one that transforms us daily. Although we may not always be aware of it, our minds are processing this information daily as we navigate the battlefield of hope and despair, love and hate, resentment and forgiveness. It is a world of opposites that we battle with, and it is a world that many of us call reality. While we can choose not to have that be our reality, we are bombarded by the experiences and events that shape our "reality" through our attention to it.

"Living from Your Soul," a course that Neil Donald Walsh moderates, has taught me how the process of creating our reality really works. More importantly, it has shown me how we choose to lose our connection with our source of being. In the course, I have come to learn about and experience how the mechanics of the mind and the system of the soul work. I would encourage any of you, if interested, to consider finding him online or to look for his books: *Conversations with God*, *The Only Thing That Matters*, and *What God Said*, in addition to many others.

When we consider the idea of "taking our temperature," what we are doing is checking in with our internal nature, our divine spark, or how we feel at any given moment. If you are not doing it daily, I highly recommend you consider it. If we cannot experience the feeling, we become numb to what is happening around us on a daily basis. If we cannot feel, we cannot provide the necessary medicine to help in the healing. If we cannot feel, we cannot celebrate the moments of joy and love that permeate our lives daily. If we cannot feel, we are paralyzed.

When being paralyzed affects our life (as it does to all of us at times), it means there is no movement. If there is no movement, there is no expression of energy and there is no emotion.

E(energy)=motion

I would like to suggest that emotion is the key to our ability to live a healthy life. Without it, we are paralyzed. I have had many, many years of trying to maintain a state of being without emotion (just ask my wife), thinking this would lead to spiritual growth. For twenty years I tried to exercise my mental powers to achieve a higher state of awareness. Although I achieved awareness and knowledge of many spiritual truths, the experience of those truths were not felt or experienced, they were just ideas in my mind. At the time, it made perfect sense to me. I thought that because I was not experiencing feelings (things associated with the physical body), I must be living a spiritual existence.

What I've come to learn is that by not expressing the truths I had come to know, I had in fact created a self-paralysis with no movement. I was just somebody who thought he was really spiritual and smart :-). If we try to ignore or limit our connection with the body and emotion, we limit our experience. If we deny this connection of spirit and body, we limit our experience. I now believe we were put here to experience it all.

What I have learned is that with emotion, life is more fun and interesting, and I am more passionate, caring and loving. It is the emotion, created by my thought, which causes a reaction. That reaction is the energy that creates activity and motion, and without it, there is no movement. If there were no emotion I would not be able to write this book, get up in the morning, or do anything. Emotion is the power that drives us and therefore, emotion plays an important part in the lives we live.

If we were to apply the idea of emotion to the loss of a loved one, we would have a very powerful story to tell. In loss, we feel our connection to so many things have been altered or changed and in some cases ended. This emotional roller coaster can take us to places we never dreamed of.

When my dad died, I remember crying from a place inside me I had never felt before, suggesting a depth of being that I had not been aware of before. When I have witnessed the agony and pain associated with the loss of a child, I am instantly aware of a depth of being, a place of connection so strong it challenges our connection with life itself. In this place of an emotion so strong, we consider for a moment whether we should even go on with our own life. I find it interesting that in most cases, the response is to move through it, to choose life over death, to choose hope in the midst of despair, to choose love over fear. Although it is hard to witness, to me this is perhaps the most significant evidence we have here on earth as to the power of our connection. We are connected to something greater than ourselves. We are connected to a love greater than anything we can experience here on earth, and we are all connected in the same way.

Many years ago, a friend in funeral service began presenting butterfly pins to their families. He shared with me the significance of how having this pin and wearing it in memory of their loved one provided families with both a visible and a meaningful sign of their connection in their journey together towards healing. Although it took me a few years to do it myself with our dove pins, this idea speaks to the many ways we can use an emotional experience to help move people towards healing. In our case, wearing the dove pin represents honoring the memory of their loved one. Within their family and community, whenever they are seen wearing the pin, it connects them in that thought. The pin is a physical reminder a symbol that they share the connection, thereby creating a new experience and emotion. In fact, when complete strangers see another wearing a butterfly or dove pin at the grocery store, or anywhere in public, it connects them in an even larger communal way. It is, and has been, a powerful and supportive way to help people feel safe in the movement and transition to their "new normal."

The energy associated with emotion is very strong and one that can be very difficult to embrace. It will cause us to move out of our comfort zone, and it will challenge us to what feels like a breaking point. It will feel large, in charge, and scary at times, but it has its purpose. It is there to move us toward something new. It is there to make us choose. It is there for our own good, to shock us out of our old patterns. It is there to be embraced and it will move us towards love.

The dilemma in all of this is that we have a choice.

In the many years I devoted to limiting emotion in my life, I was in a constant war with myself. In my new experience of embracing and choosing emotion (e=motion) I have blossomed to do many new things and have grown in many ways. It has been challenging, and I do fall off course. But if I were to have to do it over again, I would choose the course of energy and motion.

I have always loved the quote "When in life have you learned the most, when everything was easy or when you were most challenged?" In my experience, all of my major growth has taken place in change and movement from one place to another. Perhaps that is why I chose funeral service. Is there any other experience that challenges us to move from one place to another that is more profound? I think not.

Chapter Twenty

Freedom

"Go out, go out I beg you and taste the beauty of the wild. Behold the miracle of the earth with all the wonder of a child."
—Edna Jaques

A good friend offered me a thought she had after reading this book, and it goes like this: "There are times when we want to shield the ones we love from pain. But the only true way to healing is through our pain. It is through our connection to those we have lost that we are able to find a peace in our hearts. It is through our connection that we ultimately find our peace".

She also went on to say, "Connection exists in life, in death, and all places in between."

I am personally very grateful for her input and openness because it reflects her willingness to embrace her connection and transition through life. It shows her willingness to live a life of emotion, experience, living in the moment, with an openness to change and growth in the midst of personal pain. A close and personal love was taken from her just a short time ago as it will and has happened to all of us. It is apparent that it is a challenge and a difficult transition as we work to understand the perplexity of life and death as we navigate our time, moment to moment, day to day. It is apparent that it is hard to embrace a new normal in forging new relationships while maintaining ones of old. Yet, I am confident that can and will find a way. I am confident for her because she has acknowledged that the only true way to healing is through her pain. It is this simple truth, as difficult as it may seem at times, that will set all of us free.

> *Connection exists in life, in death, and all places in between.*

"Set yourself free from anything that might

hinder you in becoming the person you want to be. Free yourself from the uncertainties about your abilities or the worth of your dreams, from the fears that you may not be able to achieve them or that they won't be what you wanted.

Set yourself free from the past. The good things from yesterday are still yours in memory; the things you want to forget you will, for tomorrow is only a sunrise away. Free yourself from regret or guilt, and promise to live this day as fully as you can.

Set yourself free from the expectations of others, and never feel guilty or embarrassed if you do not live up to their standards. You are most important to yourself; live by what you feel is best and right for you. Others will come to respect your integrity and honesty.

Set yourself free to simply be yourself, and you will soar higher than you've ever dreamed."

Living and Dying

– Edmund O'Neil[5]

5 http://www.inspirationpeak.com/cgi-bin/stories.
cgi?record=112

Chapter Twenty One

Listen

"The earth has music for those who listen."
—George Santayana

Where do we go from here? What can we do now? If we see love in our everyday life, the world becomes a loving world. If we see hatred and suffering in our life, the world becomes one filled with suffering and hatred.

Reflect on our connection with how we get where we are, and where we are going and go there.

Reflect on our connection with emotions and how we feel and live a life of feeling

Reflect on the effect of our thoughts and how they affect the energy and connection in our world and become a participant

Reflect on how our connection in our world is created by our experience in our world.

Reflect on the connection of thought and emotion.

Reflect on your connection to all things and places.

Reflect on your connection to memories and the affect they have on you, in your world

Consider that we may need to create a new version of ourselves. At any time, we can redefine ourselves. We get to pick.

If I Only Knew

If I knew it would be the last time that I'd see you fall asleep, I would tuck you in more tightly and pray the Lord, your soul to keep.

If I knew it would be the last time that I see you walk out the door, I would give you a hug and kiss and call you back for one more.

If I knew it would be the last time I'd hear your voice lifted up in praise, I would video tape each action and word, so I could play them back day after day.

If I knew it would be the last time I could spare an extra minute to stop and say "I love you," instead of assuming you would KNOW I do.

If I knew it would be the last time I would be there to share your day, well I'm sure you'll have so many more, so I can let just this one slip away.

For surely there's always tomorrow to make up for an oversight, and we always get a second chance to make everything just right.

There will always be another day to say "I love you," and certainly there's another chance to say our "Anything I can do?"

But just in case I might be wrong, and today is all I get, I'd like to say how much I love you and I hope we never forget.

Tomorrow is not promised to anyone, young or old alike, and today may be the last chance you get to hold your loved one tight.

So if you're waiting for tomorrow, why not do it today? For if tomorrow never comes, you'll surely regret the day that you didn't take that extra time for a smile, or a kiss and you were too busy to grant someone, what turned out to be their one last wish.

So hold your loved ones close today, and whisper in their ear, tell them how much you love them and that you'll always hold them dear.

Take time to say "I'm sorry," "Please forgive me," "Thank you," or "It's okay."

And if tomorrow never comes, you'll have no regrets about today.[6]

---

6 http://www.dawnmariehuddleston.com/Poems---Books.htm

There is a time for everything and a season for everything under heaven. I believe it is our time.

Life is precious, embrace the love present in it, and share the joy it brings to shine your light in the world.

It is a journey filled with challengers and opportunity. Take its reigns and shine your light bright. For it is in the effort that all life is powered.

God Bless, and all my best to you in your journey.

My Journey

I have been planning my end of life event, my funeral for all of my professional life. I have been thinking about my own death and what life means for all my years in the funeral profession. I also have been having a wonderful experience of living in the process.

When you have the opportunity to be surrounded by death every day you are given the opportunity to reflect on the subject daily. I find that not everyone in our profession does this and very few in our world want to even consider it. But, I have found it enriching and life affirming thing to do.

As I look back, my journey has provided me the interest and motivation to research and engage in many interesting ideas, beliefs and experiences. I started my journey into the mysteries of life and death with Edgar Cayce. Edgar was considered the "father of holistic medicine" and the most documented psychic of the 20th century. For more than 40 years he gave psychic readings to thousands of seekers while in an unconscious state, diagnosing illnesses and revealing lives lived in the past and prophecies yet to come. I also enjoyed the work of Harry Houdini the famous illusionist who after his wife's death made it his mission to discredit mediums preying on the public. From there I joined a spiritualist church, read the bible cover to cover, studied the course of miracles, and have studied the works of numerous authors from Jeffrey to Abraham. More recently I've studied with Wayne Dyer, Louise Hay, Neale Donald Walsh, Greg Braden and Dr. Joe Dispenzia. I've studied Numerology, astrology, reviewed all of the charts and records that I think you can study and continue to examine the diverse and splendid world of meditation and yoga. I've completed detoxes, exercise regiments and diets and follow a regular program of holistic health treatment. I've also read cover to cover the book "Outwitting Squirrels" the cunning stratagems to reduce dramatically the egregious misappropriation of seed from your birdfeeder by squirrels (I put this here to see if you were paying attention, lol).

Why am I sharing all of this?

I'm sharing this because for me it's taken a lifetime and I'm still not done. Every day I continue to struggle with distraction, setbacks and the drama of life and those around me. My frustrations are still there but they're filtered by my knowledge and experience. And, it

I'm still not done.

is a gift. I believe we are never done with learning, that in fact we are living this experience in preparation for our next experience. It is because of this belief that I have spent so much time in my study. I want to enter the next place in my journey after my physical death as close to my spiritual reality of perfection as I can.

When it's my time to begin the next chapter of life, the next re-birth or renewal of spiritual life, I hope to be ready. I don't worry if I'm not because

I believe we have the chance to resolve any and all unfinished business when we transition over in our dying. I also believe we have a forgiving God and real forgiveness doesn't do judgment. So, no worry (okay, maybe a little). I can still recall as if yesterday the disappointment I've been to myself in the past. I'm still not content in my physical appearance. I'm still not as steady mentally, emotionally and physically as I would like. But, I see a purpose from all of it. A purpose so beautiful and full of joy and love that the past is laughable. A purpose so simple that it is hard to believe. The purpose of being, being present or living in the moment.

Being, is a topic so simple yet so large that I cannot begin to find the words to fill these pages. Being has no responsibility for others, just oneself. Being has no judgement of yourself or others, it is a place of perfect harmony unaffected by any other moment. Being just is.

In meditation I have experienced what it feels like to just be, a place of mindfulness where there is no noise or mind chatter. I have experienced it in athletics where it is commonly expressed as "being in the zone." It is in this place of quiet contemplation, peaceful silence and the connection to "that feeling" that allows us to 'just be" in the world. I cannot hold on to the concepts of being and presence in my mind when confronted with distraction and discord, but, I can hold on to the feeling. I tell you this because for many of us it is our fear of feeling that holds us back from our greatest discoveries. I see it every day in my work.

Life was designed to be felt

And we need to feel it.

Let's assume for the moment we all could "just be", quietly present for a moment, with no judgement or thoughts about anything or anyone specific. With no connection to thoughts, every time we came into contact or shared an experience we would see it as if it were the first time. If we could do this when in the presence of the dying, I believe we would feel the death of a loved one through the eyes of awe and wonder. We would experience it as one of life's most beautiful and magical moments, if we could be free of all of the baggage, judgments, fears of our past and our past experiences. It could and would open up a door to possibilities and opportunity. We could transition through life's most powerful experiences open to love, wonder and possibility. We could be free of fear, judgment, condemnation and pain.

I believe this would be a good place to start in the planning for your death. Start the journey of dying by dying to your old self. Let go of the hurt felt by unaware family and friend's actions. Let go of the fear of not being good enough. Let go of your personal disappointments and failures, chalk it up to learning life's lessons. Let go of the hesitation and procrastination and start your journey towards dying by living again. Why, if you could do something about it would you want to carry all that baggage with you when you're dying, and we're all dying?

I have spent my lifetime examining and re-examining my actions and have graduated with my masters in life. Now it's time for me to work on my doctorate. It took a lot of hard work and I wouldn't have had it any other way.

I really care about how you have your funeral and how you navigate that journey. But, I really care more about how you are going to live your life. I really care more about how the future is going to look for those following behind us. I really care about how you feel right now in the world you have created.

Planning your end of life funeral is the easy part.

About The Author

Mark K. Anthony, born and raised in Rochester NY, is the eldest son of a close family dedicated to service in the funeral profession. Mark has served his community for many years both professionally and through coaching and mentoring. Over the years, he has encouraged, and continues to encourage, others to be the best that they can be. Throughout a lifetime of hard work, dedication, self-reflection, contemplation, and questioning, he has come to know a place of peace and harmony in his life.

An intuitive personality since an early age, Mark brings a spirited and unique look into the field of funeral service. After fifty plus years of working on self he has discovered that when "in connection" with life's gifts, they all work in perfect harmony with each other. While there have been many challenges, this has allowed for a very peaceful and well balanced life.

Sharing his journey with us, Mark presents us with a firsthand look into the funeral profession, which up until recently has been veiled. It is his hope that you, the reader, will benefit from his work and openness. It is Mark's belief that we all have the capacity to heal through our choices in life, and the key is being willing.

> *I feel that we all have personal gifts in life, it just becomes a matter of how far you choose to develop them and which ones you feel most comfortable doing. I can only hope you can be willing to open yourself up to a reflective view of my profession, life, spirituality and family".*

—*Mark K. Anthony*

Appendix

Abstract

Three hundred and eighteen parent-bereaved children aged 5–17 recruited from the community and their surviving parents were interviewed at 1, 6, 13, and 25 months post-parental death about their participation in funeral related rituals and subsequent adjustment following the death. Nearly all the children attended their parent's visitation, funeral, and burial. Children from families who did not have such rituals fare less well over time. Children who reported internalizing or externalizing behavior at rituals were more likely to experience some increased problems in the first two years post-death. Children who were withdrawn or quiet during the rituals had fewer subsequent problems than children who acted out during these rituals. Visitation attendance was associated with better outcome one and two years later. The symbolism of rituals (e.g., playing a favorite song) often brings comfort to child survivors. Cremation does not appear to have any negative effect on children's outcome.

Source

Fristad, Mary A., Julie Cerel, Maria Goldman, Elizabeth B. Weller, and Ronald A. Weller. "The role of ritual in children's bereavement." OMEGA-Journal of Death and Dying 42, no. 4 (2001): 321-339.

IF YOU'RE A FAN OF THIS BOOK, PLEASE TELL OTHERS...

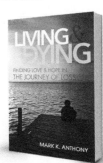

- Write about it on your blog, Twitter, Facebook, and LinkedIn pages.

- Suggest it to friends, neighbors, and family.

- When you're in a bookstore, ask if they carry the book. The book is available through all major distributors, so any bookstore that does not stock the book can easily stock it.

- Write a positive review on www.amazon.com.

- Purchase additional copies to give away as gifts.

- Connect with us on Facebook: https://www.facebook.com/ AnthonyFuneralChapels

- To order this book in bulk quantity, you may contact the publisher directly at: www.ahigherlife.com info@ahigherlife.com

The Anthony Family

We all experience loss—but how do you move forward? How can you celebrate the past without holding on to it? How can you embrace hope and joy for what lies ahead?

Mark Anthony offers consulting and coaching. Mark offers a unique understanding of death. His coaching and consulting can help you:

■ Learn to "let go" and still "hold on"

■ Make connections that support you

■ How to Un-Stuck yourself in the grief process

■ Acknowledge the good that enriches your soul

"Grief does not change you...it reveals you."
—John Green

Create Healing Experiences

In the depth of early grief, you might think that it would be "easier" to just take care of things as simply—and as quickly—as possible. But easier—especially in this circumstance—simply isn't better. You must set the stage for the future by giving your family and friends the opportunity to start the healing process. As you begin your journey on this new path, you do not venture out alone. Our caring and skilled staff are with you at all points in this process offering support and direction. We also do not stop with our support at the end of our time together it continues for years. It is our commitment and assistance in creating healing experiences that sets us apart.

Contact us at:
Anthony Chapels
(585) 244-0770
www.anthonychapels.com